Young Writers 2003 Creative Writing Competition For Secondary Schools

From Devon & Cornwall
Edited by Liz Thornbury

Disclaimer

Young Writers has maintained every effort
to publish stories that will not cause offence.

Any stories, events or activities relating to individuals
should be read as fictional pieces and not construed
as real-life character portrayal.

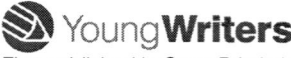

First published in Great Britain in 2005 by:
Young Writers
Remus House
Coltsfoot Drive
Peterborough
PE2 9JX
Telephone: 01733 890066
Website: www.youngwriters.co.uk

All Rights Reserved

© Copyright Contributors 2005

SB ISBN 1 84602 284 3

Foreword

Young Writers was established in 1991 and has been passionately devoted to the promotion of reading and writing in children and young adults ever since. The quest continues today. *Young Writers* remains as committed to engendering the fostering of burgeoning poetic and literary talent as ever.

This year, *Young Writers* are happy to present a dynamic and entertaining new selection of the best creative writing from a talented and diverse cross section of some of the most accomplished secondary school writers around. Entrants were presented with four inspirational and challenging themes.

'Myths And Legends' gave pupils the opportunity to adapt long-established tales from mythology (whether Greek, Roman, Arthurian or more conventional eg The Loch Ness Monster) to their own style.

'A Day In The Life Of …' offered pupils the chance to depict twenty-four hours in the lives of literally anyone they could imagine. A hugely imaginative wealth of entries were received encompassing days in the lives of everyone from the top media celebrities to historical figures like Henry VIII or a typical soldier from the First World War.

Finally 'Short Stories', in contrast, offered no limit other than the author's own imagination while 'Hold The Front Page' provided the ideal opportunity to challenge the entrants' journalistic skills, asking them to provide a newspaper or magazine article on any subject of their choice.

T.A.L.E.S. From Devon & Cornwall is ultimately a collection we feel sure you will love, featuring as it does the work of the best young authors writing today.

Contents

Camborne Science & Community College, Camborne
Jasmine Harrington (11)	1
Laureen Hodge (12)	2
Chelsea Dennis (12)	3
Kassey Lambourne (12)	4
Jed Clemens (12)	5
Oliver Nidds (12)	6
Sarah Clark (12)	7
Sharna Powell-Thomas (12)	8
Tommy Salmon (12)	9
David Gundry (13)	10
Hannah McNamee (12)	11
Sarah Wright (12)	12

Edgehill College, Bideford
Rowan Styles (11)	13
Jessica Berry (11)	14
Stephanie Green (11)	15
Brisa Sanders-Hill (11)	16
Nicola Grant (12)	17
Victoria Charles (13)	18
John Hodgson (13)	19
Michelle Smith (13)	20
Roseanne Bromell (14)	21
Shonagh Dowdle (14)	22
Sarah Edwards (14)	23
Miranda Gent (14)	24
Chantal Moore (14)	25
Philip Watson (14)	26

Estover Community College, Plymouth
Clare Rowley (13)	27
Daniel Wade (12)	28
Sasha Holden (12)	29
David Bulpett (12)	30
Sam Wooldridge (13)	31
Alex Lang (13)	32
Phillip Marshall (13)	33

John Drake (15)	34
Daniel Harvey (14)	35
Lawrence Bassett (14)	36
David Carron (13)	37
Kayleigh Clarke (13)	38
Charlotte Clarke (14)	39
Benjamin Mitchell (12)	40
Chris Miles (14)	41
Abby Cocking (14)	42
Robert Crispin (14)	43
Luke Nicol (14)	44
David Gardener (14)	45
Michael Davies (14)	46
Troy Hill (14)	47
Michael Raven (14)	48
Corey Marshall (14)	49
Jessica Loomes (14)	50
Amelia Downing (15)	51
Daniel Loveless (14)	52
Charlotte Nicholson (14)	53
Megan Chamberlaine (14)	54
Nicola Taylor (14)	55
Erin Horrell (13)	56
Zoe Roberts (13)	57
Dan Tucker (14)	58
Sophie Seldon (12)	59
Christopher Brooking (13)	60
Jessica Veacock (12)	61
Natasha Arnold (13)	62
Emma Humphries (13)	63
Amy Mouncher (13)	64
Marek Vincenc (13)	65
Steven France (14)	66
Danny Kendall (13)	67

Hillside Special School, Plymouth

Georgia Ball (12)	68
Darren Davis (13)	69
Craig Knight (12)	70
Gareth Lewis (13)	71
Raymond Steyn (13)	72

Nikita Wood (13) — 73
Steven Lilley (13) — 74
Ryan Harvey (13) — 75
Daniel Smith (13) — 76
Adam Krisht (13) — 77
Jamie Hosking (12) — 78
Lewis Joyce (13) — 79
Sarah Symons (14) — 80
Josieanne Thyer (14) — 81
Thomas Channing (14) — 82
Rebecca Armitage (14) — 83
Dimitri Coxon (13) — 84
Laura Colmer (14) — 85

St Ives School, St Ives
Phoebe Gwillim-Jones (12) — 86
Sophie Vallance (12) — 87
Steven Smith (12) — 88
Timmy Halliday (11) — 89
Hatty Phillips (12) — 90
Katie Williams (11) — 91
Peter Trevorrow (Autistic) (11) — 92
Pippa Monies (12) — 93
Matt Hobson (12) — 94
Samuel Jackson (12) — 95
Billy Curtis (12) — 96
Rebecca Knee (12) — 97
Chris Pugh (12) — 98
Toni Chaplin (12) — 99
Charlie Rudge (12) — 100
Becky Nankervis (12) — 101

St James' High School, Exeter
Reece Mills (13) — 102
Jodie Lemon (13) — 103
Timothy Hannah (13) — 104
Misha Vertkin (13) — 105
Chloe Meredith (13) — 106
Jade Ashelford (13) — 107
Joshua Grimes (13) — 108
Terri Cainey (13) — 109

James Parmenter (13)   110

St Luke's High School, Exeter
Simon Johns (14)   111
Lucy Foote (14)   112
Josh Clarkin (15)   113
Luke Plain (14)   114
Kylie Hardwick (14)   115
Deborah Kellaway (14)   116
Jordan Westcott (13)   117

Torpoint Community School, Torpoint
Ruby Fuller (11)   118
Thomas Harry (12)   119
Amy Fishwick (12)   120
Ben Ayres (12)   121
Lewis Allan (12)   122
Megan Marshall (11)   123
Sophie Palmer (14)   124
Michael Ives (12)   125
Bethanie Dwyer (14)   126
Sarah Day (14)   127
Lily Gillman (15)   128
David Flint (15)   129
Leanne Stevens (15)   130
Yasmin Carson (14)   131
Emily Hall (15)   132
Beth Hunt (15)   133
Callie Jenkins (14)   134
Maddison Nixon (14)   135
Jack Langley (14)   136
Paul Creek (14)   137
Josh Grant (14)   138
Louise Cordrey (14)   139
Dean Owen (14)   140
Ben Surman (14)   141
Cleo Summers (14)   142
Tom Payne (13)   143
Sam Hough (13)   144
Charlotte Goodacre (12)   145
Chelsee Gill (13)   146

Nicole Talbot (13)	147
Forrest Kernan (12)	148
Adam Stone (13)	149
Racheal Phelps (13)	150
Michael Osborne (12)	151
Jade Walkden (13)	152
Luke Jones (13)	153
Louise Bond (12)	154
Chelsey Clarke (12)	155
Hannah Rosson (12)	156
Lucy Duncan (13)	157
Tom Willcocks (15)	158
Cali Fielding (15)	160
James Gibbs (13)	161
Stephanie Tweedie (12)	162
Alicia Keise (13)	163
Danielle Williams (13)	164
Amy Maynard (12)	165
James Hough (13)	166
Matthew Beadnall (13)	167
Carys Owen (12)	168
Alex Bird (12)	169
Scott Redding (13)	170
Alice Edlin (12)	171
Benjamin Applegate (12)	172
Louis Ryan (13)	173
Chris Waterfield (12)	174
James Bevan (13)	175
Will Bennett (13)	176
Adam Curtin (13)	177
Gemma Viant (15)	178
Mark Floyd (15)	180
Sarah Killingsworth (14)	181

Torquay Boys' Grammar School, Torquay

Matt Barrett (14)	182
Shaun Cockman (14)	183
Ben Howitt (11)	184
Ben Sebastian (12)	185
Matthew Derbyshire (11)	186
David Gabb (12)	187

James Chatterton (12)	188
Jack Lang (12)	189
Ethan Luke (12)	190
Barcley Spicer-Jenkins (11)	191
Craig Murch (12)	192
Joe Arnold (12)	193
Tim McLennan (14)	194
Kai Feller (13)	195
Max Russell (14)	196
James Hardy (14)	197
Jono Beardsmore (14)	198
Joseph Brook (14)	199
Rhys Lewis (14)	200
Jack Staples (13)	201
Alex Hambis (13)	202
Sam Burnham (12)	203
Tom Colley (12)	204
Joe Vincent (13)	205
Alex Finn (13)	206
Michael Wilby (12)	207
Luke Jeffery (13)	208
Harrhy James (13)	209
Henry Irvine (13)	210
Arun Allen (12)	211
Matt Thompson (13)	212
William Saunders (12)	213
James Sutherland (12)	214
Jonathan Munro (12)	215
David Burke (11)	216
Jordan Bright (12)	217
Gordon Watton (12)	218
Luke Hayward (12)	219
Anthony Savage (12)	220
Peter Dawkins (11)	221
John Richards (12)	222
John Ware (11)	223
Luke Lake (12)	224
Michael Barrington (12)	225
Nick Aitchison (12)	226
Adam Robinson (12)	227
Chris Gossage (14)	228
Harry Richardson (14)	229

Matt Scott (12) 230
Daniel Garswood (12) 231
Gareth Jones (13) 232
Matthew Thornton (13) 233
Max Leaman (12) 234
Sam Hurst (12) 235
Simon White (13) 236

The Creative Writing

Creak

One night, my mum and dad had gone out for the evening and left me in the care of an aunt who I'd never met before. She had this really big, creepy, old house, so I was a bit scared. She went to bed early, so I stayed downstairs to watch television.

Creak. I heard something. *Ah, it'll just be Aunt getting a drink,* I thought, so I went back to watching the television.

Creak! This time it was louder. I shook my head, thinking I was imagining it.

Creak! I *definitely* heard something. I went upstairs. 'Aunt, are you OK?' I asked into the nothingness.

No reply.

She'll be asleep, I thought. I checked the room I was sleeping in. No one. I went to bed. Then I woke up in the middle of the night when I heard a large *creak!* I jumped out of bed and onto the landing. I grabbed a candle from the bookcase and went to explore. I could see nothing. Then I heard a noise from downstairs. I raced down the stairs and into the living room. All I could hear was *creak, creak, creak.* I was frightened. Then suddenly I heard a voice.

'Jasmine, could you get me some oil for my bedroom door?' asked Aunt.

It had been her all along.

'Sure,' I replied, reassured that I didn't find anything but an old *creaky* door.

Jasmine Harrington (11)
Camborne Science & Community College, Camborne

The Blue Flu!

As I looked out of the coach window, the school started to get smaller and smaller. Suddenly I had a spine-chilling feeling that this summer camp wasn't to be fun at all!

I'm Violet and I'm a caring, achieving eleven-year-old. I live in New Orleans. I have two best friends, Sam and Andrea. Andrea and I are a bit envious of Sam because she is rich and has designer clothes.

We were travelling on a stuffy coach on practically the hottest day of the year. We soon entered the countryside. A blood-curdling sensation crept over me. Everything was blue!

Soon we arrived at the campsite. The trees' warning calls filled the icy air - 'Stay away!'

The next morning Sam didn't get up. She stayed in bed all day with a fever.

That evening there was a newsflash. A new superbug had been discovered. Sam had the blue flu.

That night, Andrea and I came up with a cure for the blue flu. We were going to the toilet block when we came across a soft humming. We followed the humming and found a little red flower. We got the flower tested and it had micro-organisms in it which could cure the blue flu!

I've always wanted to save the world and I did! If you want to really achieve something have faith in yourself and you'll achieve your goal!

Laureen Hodge (12)
Camborne Science & Community College, Camborne

Life As A Banana!

27th June:
 Yippee, I have finally grown and I can now start a new life. Today I am going to try and make some new friends, hopefully they will be as nice as the other friends I had, they were extremely nice to me, they even treated me day and night.

5th July:
 Doesn't anyone like me or anything? I have been trying to make a new friend for over a week and no one will be my friend. I have tried a tree, grass, trampoline and even a battery! They are so selfish, they don't even talk. It looks like I'll have to be friends with a monkey, even though that is my worst nightmare!

10th August:
 I have finally achieved my mission. I am now friends with a monkey! I have been singing my favourite songs to him, including 'It's Bananas, B, A, N, A, N, A, S!' I think he really enjoyed it. Have I told you that his name is Bob? He is really nice, even though I get the feeling that I am going to be eaten within a week!

17th August:
 I am really scared now, even my beautiful yellow skin is going black! I am only worried because I have a gut feeling that I am going to be eaten around about ... now! *Argh!* Told you. My life is over. I was about to sing another one of my favourite songs, 'Molla bing, molla bang, molla bing, molla bang!' I'm dead!

Chelsea Dennis (12)
Camborne Science & Community College, Camborne

24-Hour Story Of A Slave Girl

One day a slave girl woke up and she was packed very tightly in the hold of a ship. She was in old rags with holes that someone had tried to sew back together. She had sore cuts and blisters.

All that she had to eat was one bowl of soggy, watered-down porridge to last her a whole day.

She did not like the sailors because they were nasty and very foul-mouthed. They spoke to her like a piece of dirt they'd seen on the floor.

They made her lay in other people's mess and her own, they would not even let her clean herself up. She was tied up to a post with eight other people.

She could not wait until she got to wherever she was going. That was what the slave girl I was watching was doing.

Kassey Lambourne (12)
Camborne Science & Community College, Camborne

The Legend Of The Boy Who Was Half Monkey

I was in the jungle looking for types of monkeys and I found a family of orang-utans. One was eating strange fruits, a purple apple, and then he stuck his tongue out at me and jumped on me, but didn't hit me. He bit me and my hand went purple like the fruit. The orang-utan jumped off and went back on the tree. I quickly ran home because of the bite, then I collapsed.

I woke up in my bed, but I felt different. I went to my mirror. *Argh!* I'd got a tail, my face was hairy, I was a monkey! It was that orang-utan. It was night and I had to keep my parents from seeing me. I was hungry so I went downstairs to get some crisps. I walked down and got a banana instead. I could climb trees, so I climbed but slipped and landed in the dog food, then Patch, my dog, came out.

He growled at me so I quickly climbed up the tree and saw a man getting hit. I jumped off and ran. The guy beating him had a bat and hit the man with it, so I grabbed some mangoes and threw them and chased him off. Then I ran to the man, he was a medicine man and for helping him he gave me a cure.

Jed Clemens (12)
Camborne Science & Community College, Camborne

A Day In The Life Of A Teacher

Beep, beep as the alarm goes off. Another day of pestering kids bothering me, asking for help, being cheeky. I'm not looking forward to today. Oh well, another day, more money. Breakfast of Weetabix and coffee. Maybe they will be good today but I doubt it.

In school and a bad start. Bob and George had a fight and I've had to call their parents. They aren't pleased at all. They even try to blame me. I mean, how can they do that? I stopped the fight. Maybe they wanted me to leave them to tear each other to pieces, I'll let that happen next time.

Into registration and they are already not listening to me. How am I supposed to do the register without them answering. Finally I get them quiet. Oh no, the firebell's going off. All outside now and be quick about it.

All outside and one person is missing. What's going to happen?

Oliver Nidds (12)
Camborne Science & Community College, Camborne

The Dragon And The Wolf Of The Night

It's a stormy night outside my cave. I can hear the thunder roll and the lightning strike. Every night a wolf comes out to explore, he sniffs around, but when he howls, lightning strikes.

Tonight the lightning has already struck every blade of grass, every bird in the sky. The wind is getting stronger, it grows; the wolf is out, wandering, as he does. I can see sprites (real and strong lightning, positive lightning with red and blue strands, dancing in the night). *Run wolf, run, get to safety.* What am I saying? I don't care for that pathetic little wolf.

The lightning, the thunder, the wind, what a sight. I am seeing all the storm's delight, striking and rolling, blowing around, but as I sit and watch, I can't stop feeling sorry for the wolf; he has no family, I think he is scared, scared of the sun and the day.

The storm is a long storm as it strikes two trees. A fire, a roaring fire has started, blazing over the land.

I am scared of fire. I am a dragon of the air not fire. The fire dances, dances in the wind and spreads over the land. It blazes and it dances, but it won't stop, instead it comes closer.

I close my eyes and wait, wait for the flames of the roaring fire to burn me, but nothing. I open my eyes and there's the wolf. Thank you my friend, he smiles and he is gone, gone up in flames. All that is left is a pile of ashes.

Sarah Clark (12)
Camborne Science & Community College, Camborne

A Day In The Life Of A Cheetah Who Was Raised By A Girl

6am: I let my dog out for a run. I took her around the shed five times.

I heard a noise over the wall that I didn't recognise, it sounded like a cheep, cheep noise. I thought it was a bird but when I looked over the wall, I saw it was a baby cheetah. It was looking up at me. Then, at that moment, I knew it was lost, but how had it got this far away from home? I picked it up and took it to show my family.

They said, 'Where did you get that from?'

I said, 'I found it down by the wall. Can I keep it, please?' I begged.

They said nicely, 'But it's a wild animal. When it grows up it will want to eat everyone in town.'

I said plainly, 'I will train it to be kind and not eat everyone in town. I will train it to be friendly to everyone. So can I keep it, please?' I pleaded.

In the end they gave in and said, 'Yes, you can keep it, but you have to housetrain it too.'

'OK,' I said.

The cheetah could grow up with me, my two sisters, Mum, Dad, my fish and my dog as well. It grew up to be kind, friendly and housetrained just like I promised my family.

Sharna Powell-Thomas (12)
Camborne Science & Community College, Camborne

A Day In The Life Of A Football

It was 8am and suddenly a light appeared. I was taken out of the cupboard. I remembered that there was a match, England Vs Germany. I was taken out onto a field and I was kicked around in front of the biggest crowd I have ever seen.

The game started. I was being passed around and finally I was touched by David Beckham! Ahh! David Beckham!

The day just kept getting better because England scored. It was injury time for the second half, but then England scored again - 2-0! The whistle went and I was taken into the smelly changing rooms.

10 minutes later I was taken out to the fresh air again. Germany kicked off this time but straight away England snatched me off Herpia and crossed me into their box. John Terry headed me into their net. It was an early goal.

It was all going well until suddenly I was hit so hard by Oliver Kahn I felt a sharp pain. I had been punctured!

Where was I? It was dark. Was I back in the cupboard or was I in a bin?

Tommy Salmon (12)
Camborne Science & Community College, Camborne

Ghost

His footsteps echoed around the imposing walls. Rain drove down. The lamp flickered and was extinguished.

Andrew kicked through the puddles, soaking his brand new jeans. He looked at his watch, eleven o'clock. In his mind he ran through excuses for his mum. He was well over an hour late and he hadn't arrived home yet. A car raced by, spraying water from the road, soaking him.

He kicked a plastic bottle along the road, but it fell into a gutter. The mannequins in the shop fronts watched him with plain, staring eyes. Something about their posture and the cold night brought an unwelcome shiver to Andrew's spine.

A ghostly figure appeared ahead of him. Andrew stood stunned and fearful. He watched the ghostly figures gliding around the streets. The ghosts were illuminated with a blood-red glow. He backed against a wall, hiding in the shadows.

He heard screaming. A woman, about twenty, was being dragged by her leg through the street, just a few yards away. The ghosts turned and, with wicked smiles, tore apart their victim. Andrew stopped himself from crying out when one of the monsters tore out a particularly gruesome part of the woman's intestines and carelessly discarded it. Andrew edged backwards silently until he was wedged in a dark corner, back against a cash machine. He didn't breathe. He waited a minute. Had they gone? Did they know he was there? He breathed heavily, though he tried to avoid it. He closed his eyes.

David Gundry (13)
Camborne Science & Community College, Camborne

The Journey Of Death For A Slave

There is a large ship coming through the dark fog. I do not want it to be what I think it is, but it is. What am I going to do? Men, men with pale skin. They are pulling and pushing us into the place we all fear, the hold, full with dark air and the smell of death. I shall live. I shall live. My older sister has been put on the same boat as me, I have to live for her. We're nearly there, not long to go. I have not thought too much about what will happen when we get there.

There the air is full of dust and dirt. This was the one that I had hoped for, but it's nowhere as good as I remember. Life's unfair.

A man starts to speak. I do not know what he is saying. I do not know.

Then I shout, 'Stop, stop.'

Now my sister speaks, she has not spoken the whole way here. She says, 'Do not worry, do not worry.'

I do not worry, she did, now she is dead. She killed herself in the bathroom where I work and live. The days shall get easier.

Hannah McNamee (12)
Camborne Science & Community College, Camborne

A Day In Pain For An African Slave

My name is Zeta and I am only 10 years old. I need to get out of this terrifying ship. It is so disgusting in here. Imagine a slave (or cargo to the white people) going to the toilet sitting down on the ground, then you would get soaked and the people beside you would get wet as well as you. Or maybe excretion, having to put up with it for a year.

Please remember that I am away from home and missing my family. You have your family. You have your home. I will never see my mother again. That's right! She has been chucked overboard. She died from a coughing illness. I need to get away from screaming, shouting and rushing pale men before I die too. I will be ever so lucky to escape from this howling ship. I am begging for help.

Sarah Wright (12)
Camborne Science & Community College, Camborne

The Wolf

I stared out at the starlit sky and marvelled at its beauty. It was a clear night and I could hear the calling of other wolves and their packs. I jumped down from the rock overhanging our cave and went into it. Two brand new cubs had been born from my mate. One was jet-black in colour and the other was pure white. My mate smiled at me as I entered the den and the rest of the pack watched intently as our cubs suckled.

The next day I went out to hunt with some of the pack. We managed to bring down a young deer, a good kill for the day. We ate some ourselves and then brought the rest back for my mate and our cubs. I sent out Bran, my best friend, to patrol our den. He came back later and said that Man was hunting in the forest, heading straight for our den! I growled a warning to my mate; we picked up a cub each by the scruff of their necks and the pack moved out. We stayed for the afternoon in amongst the trees and when the humans had gone we returned to the cave.

That night I stood on the overhanging rock, lifted my grey muzzle and howled. The world that we lived in was truly magnificent.

Rowan Styles (11)
Edgehill College, Bideford

Bucksford Manor

I waved out the window, a tear running down my chin. I felt that a chunk of my heart had just disappeared. I felt alone. I didn't want to leave my home and family, but I knew it was what my parents wanted, me to be sent off to boarding school - Bucksford Manor.

After five hours in a smoky train I finally arrived. It was a small town called Bucksford; so it made sense that I was staying in Bucksford Manor. I briskly walked off the train and I noticed a small sign reading *Bucksford Manor - Left.* I walked on.

Suddenly I was there. I thought it would have taken at least an hour, but it took ten minutes. I took a deep breath and my eyes captured the large building in front of me. I felt like an ant gazing up at an elephant. The bricks were rusty reds and the grass was cut to perfection. Also I noticed that there were no sounds of children or bells. Butterflies flew round in my stomach. I walked in gingerly, then I heard patters of footsteps.

'You must be Elizabeth, the new girl?' a confident girl asked.

'Yes ... I am,' I replied slowly.

'You look pale. Don't worry. I'll look after you.'

'Thank you,' I exclaimed.

She showed me my room and I soon settled in. I decided boarding school wasn't that scary after all.

Jessica Berry (11)
Edgehill College, Bideford

An Interesting Find

We were trudging up the hill after a long day at school when I heard a cry.

'Help me!'

I turned towards Jess and said, 'Sorry?'

'I didn't say anything!' she exclaimed.

'Oh,' I shrugged.

'Help me,' I heard again.

'Did you hear that?'

'No, nothing.'

We kept on walking in silence until I said, 'Well, I've erm ... got homework to do, so I'll see you tomorrow. Bye!' I slowly walked back to where I had heard the noise and when she was out of sight, I asked, 'Hello, anyone there?' I nervously brushed away the leaves to reveal an old computer. I searched the hedgerow but there was nothing else to be seen. I wanted to find out more, so somehow I managed to get it to my room in one piece! I'm a whizz at computers so within 2 minutes it was on, up and working.

'Hello.'

I jumped. It was definitely talking. 'Hello,' I said.

There was no reply, so I typed *hello*.

'What are you called?' it asked.

I typed *Steph*.

'Hello Steph!'

This was so exciting! I was having a conversation with a computer! We talked for ages about its previous owners and how it could talk.

'Are you intelligent?' I asked.

'Yes of course, I have the whole Internet inside me!'

'Well ...' I started. Within 10 minutes the deal was done. I had saved it. So now it would save me, by being a friend and completing every piece of my homework!

Stephanie Green (11)
Edgehill College, Bideford

A Scary Night

It was a dark, stormy, spooky night and Lucy Grove was lying awake in bed. The storm was keeping her up and she couldn't go to sleep. Suddenly there was a creak and the door gradually opened. From behind the door came a black figure that crept over to Lucy's bed. She screamed, but it didn't go away. She screamed again but it just seemed to get closer and closer. Trembling, Lucy pulled the bed covers over her head and shut her eyes, hoping it would all go away. She heard deafening lightning strike and pulled the covers tighter. The window flew open and Lucy was extremely frightened. She could sense the figure coming closer and closer, and Lucy knew it was going to grab the covers from her and do something horrible! She anxiously waited and waited, but nothing happened. She gave it a few more seconds and still nothing.

Carefully Lucy pulled the covers away from her face. The figure had gone. She thought it must have been a nightmare. Her heart was beating fast and sweat was running from her forehead. Just to make sure the figure had gone, Lucy slowly climbed out of bed and made her way towards the closed door. She shakily pushed the door open and there was no one there. Lucy breathed a sigh of relief and turned round to get back into bed but when she turned she saw the figure standing right in front of her.

Brisa Sanders-Hill (11)
Edgehill College, Bideford

A Dog's Life

There are 8 basic rules to keeping your dog happy. If you break just one of these rules (as my owner did) you end up with one unhappy, angry dog. Take me for instance. I was perfectly happy until that *kennel* showed up, but anyway, more about that later. Here are my rules for a *dog's life*.

1) The principles of Feng Shui - a dog has got to be able to personalise his home in order to feel at harmony with it and, besides, humans have no taste
2) The Canine Five Elements - ball, stick, bowl, bone and biscuit
3) Career development - what's the point in having a dog if you don't let it fetch your newspaper?
4) A nose for business - dogs need to read
5) Obedience classes - it is important that your owner learns discipline
6) Health and happiness - all dogs need a balanced diet
7) Further afield - make sure your dog has enough space
8) Tactics of location - dogs have got to be able to lie where they want, even if it is in an inconvenient place

But unfortunately, it's on rules 1 and 7 where my human went wrong - just because I accidentally raised a leg to his sofa, I am now banned from the house. Forced to live in a kennel ... how humiliating ...

In this story you will discover how much dogs are valued, and just how badly humans cope without them ...

Nicola Grant (12)
Edgehill College, Bideford

Lightning Tells All

It was raining heavily when David Brigham, after collecting firewood all day, opened the door leading into the abandoned hut, which was a refuge for a group of lost journalists. It was their only hope of survival.

It creaked loudly and the cameraman, John Reese, welcomed him. 'How much have you collected then?' said Reese smiling.

'Not a lot, it was all damp. I had to go into the cover of the forest to find decent stuff,' he said. 'Right, I'm going to try and get dry.'

'OK,' John replied.

David and John had been sent to Latvia to do research on the forests, but their trip had been disrupted by armed gangs of terrorists who didn't like them.

By 9pm the rain had got steadily worse. It was beginning to leak through the holes in the battered roof, and lightning lit up the shack and the meadow around them. Thunder rumbled over them, the hairs on the back of everyone's neck stood on end.

David had dried off and was looking out of the broken front window; he watched the strikes of lightning flash over them. A split second of daylight. What was that? Had he imagined it or had he just seen the glinting eyes of men? About 10 pairs of eyes were making their way towards the hut. He waited for another flash to check. Should he raise the alarm? Just then was an explosion of bullets and all went quiet.

Victoria Charles (13)
Edgehill College, Bideford

A Day In The Life Of A Caveman

It was early morning and Mr Ugg was sitting in the entrance to his cave, looking out over the forest and sharpening his spear on the rocks. He was going hunting soon with his fellow Uggish friends. Mr Ugg was a gentle man and leader of the Ugg tribe. One by one his warriors gathered to travel into the forest.

They set off and immediately came across a large beast that was instantly slain and brought back to the camp. It was hours of walking before a warrior said that he heard a rustle in the surrounding bushes. The group spread out, poised with spears ready. Then, out of nowhere, they were surrounded by enemies. It was an ambush. There was no escape. The enemy leader emerged from a nearby bush. It was Umba of the Stomar tribe, an arch-enemy.

'Join us and your people will be spared,' said Umba.

'I will never join you,' replied Ugg.

'Very well.'

Umba raised his hand and his men raised their spears, ready to attack. His hand began to fall when there was a roar from the mountainside. Everyone turned to look and there was a massive Ugg army charging down the hill into the forest.

'Attack!' yelled Ugg.

The warriors turned and threw their spears at the distracted enemy. A battle followed with both sides taking heavy losses until the Ugg army at last arrived and Umba himself fell to the ground.

John Hodgson (13)
Edgehill College, Bideford

Shock

Emily sat up with a start. She sobbed and her eyes were sore with sadness. She had found out just last night that Terry, her husband, was dead due to the tsunami in Thailand. Her heart mourned with sadness. Her life seemed to be empty without Terry and, just to make it worse, she kept on getting terrible stomach aches. She swept her hand along where he would lie to certify that it was true. He had gone over to Thailand to help people and now he had died in the process.

Nothing will ever be the same again, she thought to herself. *Now I shall be left a widow at the age of 24. What will people think? This is the lady whose husband died when she was 24 and she's never loved anyone since. I couldn't love anyone else,* she thought. It was impossible. Her heart was filled with sorrow.

As the day progressed, Emily remembered that she had a doctor's appointment. Walking with her head down, and dragging her feet, she went to the nearby doctor's.

As she sat in the waiting room, she thought only of Terry until her name was called and she entered the doctor's. He immediately recognised her symptoms. It was going to change her life - forever.

'Well, I think I know what is wrong with you, you are pregnant.'

'What? My husband will never see his child!' She burst into tears. She felt her life would be ruined, forever.

Michelle Smith (13)
Edgehill College, Bideford

A Writer

What to write? Another tale of a sad, lonely girl? Perhaps another love story, two people fall in love, fall out of love, then get back together. Then there are stories that are just not understandable. They're made up of similes and metaphors; the story is just rubbish. If it was written properly it wouldn't make sense anyway. I don't understand why more books should be written when there probably isn't a single person in the world who has read all the most brilliant ones anyway.

So my story is about a writer who devoted her life to writing, but never came up with anything worthwhile. Every day she sat at her desk, blank computer screen in front of her and coffee by her side. She searched high and low for inspiration but to no avail.

Then, one day, she delved deep inside her own memories. She remembered her first day at school, her mother dying when she was 10, her first love, her first broken heart, her habit of forgetting one ingredient when cooking. Suddenly it dawned on her that she was alone. She had nobody to share anything with. She looked around her living room; the wastepaper basket was overflowing with unsuccessful stories. The shelves were lifeless and the settee neat and empty. She had spent so long trying to put into words what she didn't have in her mind, she forgot what she needed to have in reality.

Roseanne Bromell (14)
Edgehill College, Bideford

Chinese Democracy - Will It Ever Be Released?

New Guns 'N' Roses Album Is Set For Release In December.

The long-awaited Guns 'N' Roses album, Chinese Democracy, still remains to be seen. Axl Rose (lead singer) has been working on the album for over 7 years and has spent over $13 million on it. Many dates have been issued by Guns 'N' Roses for the release of the album but Chinese Democracy seems yet to be unfinished! A date issued by HMV recently said that the album was due to come out on April 25th but once again it was unable to make the date.

Guns 'N' Roses, who were last seen at the MTV awards in 2002, claim that the album is very nearly finished with just the final touches to be made, like the finishing of the mixing, what songs should be on the album and the artwork.

Tommy Stinson (bass) has hinted to Creative Loafing Magazine in Atlanta that GnR may probably be touring Europe this summer, but fans seem to have very little trust in GnR touring or even releasing their album because of the delay, which has led to many fans losing interest. Fans have criticised Axl and said that the only reason Axl is not releasing the album is because he wants the attention from being abused by both his stepdad and biological father when he was a child.

A further release date for Chinese Democracy has now been issued again by Guns 'N' Roses for around December this year.

'Chinese Democracy is very close to being completed. Occasionally time is just what it takes to make a great album', says Merck Mercunaus, chief executive officer from Sanctuary Group.

So will we be seeing Guns 'N' Roses' new album in December or will it still not be finished? The fact is that nobody knows, so we will just have to wait and see, but when any information comes in we will let you know!

Shonagh Dowdle (14)
Edgehill College, Bideford

Interview With Scott Gray

This week I finally got to meet Scott Gray, the England footballer, as he trained for Euro 2008. Euro 2008 is a major tournament for any football player but at the age of 17, Scott Gray is one of the youngest players in the tournament. Scott Gray is the most handsome young man around at the moment in any standard. He has achieved many awards over the past year which have made him the celebrity he is today.

I met Scott inside the Manchester United football ground where we had coffee and biscuits and talked over his plans for the future. This was a first for me, inside a top of the league football ground and meeting with the biggest up-and-coming young footballer of the decade.

Scott, who last season played for Fulham, has now signed a contract with Manchester United for an undisclosed sum which is reputed to be around 20 million pounds.

Scott has played for the England under 21s twenty times and has scored a record number of goals, before being elected for the full England squad. Just before leaving the interview to practise with his fellow England players he said how he would like to score a record number of goals for England. At the end of the interview I wished him well for the future with Manchester United and England.

Sarah Edwards (14)
Edgehill College, Bideford

A Day In The Life Of A Jar Of Jam

My jar is standing with our platoon of preserves. The darkness surrounding me feels cool. As I say, 'store in a cool dark place', there's no breeze or blazing light as there once was. I can hear nothing of what I used to, just the occasional laughter, crash, yell or thud.

This life I now live is so tedious. The daily routine is practically invariable. At the first glimpse of light through the crack in the opening, a grubby little *thing* with five feelers grabs me and twists off my head ... in slides a shiny tool. My red juices spray and I feel strangely empty. Silently I watch my insides being eaten away.

I suppose that's one good thing ... my new diet is amazing. I weighed 454g before. Now I'm losing weight every day. Today I'm more than tomorrow, yet less than yesterday.

Sometimes I'm left out, my sticky head not properly screwed on. Occasionally buzzy things would check me out, reminding me of home, before the giants with wrinkly feelers took me away. It's depressing: I hate to whinge, but my life was so beautiful.

I remember my youth in the sun amongst my friends and family. I shouldn't think back too much. Being blistered with sugar, I am more than I was, yet every day I become less. I know one day I'll disappear.

Well, back to my platoon! This has been 'a day of my life', I am jam.

Miranda Gent (14)
Edgehill College, Bideford

Opening Scene Of A Novel Entitled 'The Missing Pieces'

Daniel walked in slowly, gazing at his mother with utter confusion and anxiety. He wondered what was so important, why she had phoned the school and requested that he come home immediately. Daniel was eager to find out why, but when he saw his mother's melancholy expression he knew he would regret hearing it.

He stopped walking when he was opposite her, with only the oak table separating them. He bowed his head and looked at the tiled kitchen floor his father had laid many years ago, not moving or saying anything until his mother told him to look her in the face.

Her eyes were swollen and overflowing with tears. Her face was blotched with red patches from where she had been crying, while her nose was constantly running. Daniel felt his gut lurch deep within him, his blood turned cold and the clock stopped ticking.

'Mum?' he mumbled very quietly and slowly, shivering as he spoke. 'What's wrong?' Daniel stared into his mother's eyes with deep affection, trying to comfort her. He longed to hug her tightly and make her happy again. She was the one who gave life to him, put up with him when he was in a mood and helped him when he was low.

'Your dad,' she began, glass beads falling uncontrollably down her puffed-up cheeks. 'He was found in his workshop this morning, d ... dead. Your f ... father was m ... murdered.'

Chantal Moore (14)
Edgehill College, Bideford

Alone

He rested his weary pen. Snatching the paper from in front of his eyes, he screwed it up tightly so that he could feel the sharp paper edges press deep into his skin, confirming he was alive. He paused, wide-eyed with cat's stare into the dark night on the other side of the window; could it be that soft whisper he cherished? But it was just the wind taunting his every thought. His feet connected with the bitter stone floor and he felt the chills despatch through to the very corners of his soul. No more writing for tonight, tear stains scarred his many discarded papers. He was somnolent but had no intention of sleeping. Just rest.

He had promised himself no more crying. He felt so stupid, weeping. *A grown man like myself should not be crying*, he told himself. He did make a feeble attempt to stop but there was no one there to tell him to grow up. He preferred the night, no prying eyes; they didn't really care, just nosy. Anyway, he didn't much care anymore for polite niceties. Why give your time for people you don't care for? He'd make his words count now. But words, he could never have said enough. He could never find the phrase or express himself from his heart, only once, words now carved in vain onto her solid gravestone. Never spoken.

Philip Watson (14)
Edgehill College, Bideford

Shipwreck Diary

Dear Diary,
 I was sailing on a galleon, but a terrible thing happened four weeks into our journey. I was going to Africa. I was so looking forward to the trip. Being a teacher was my dream. I'm 30 and not married.
 Then it happened. I was asleep when we were caught in a storm. The mast snapped. I tried desperately to get to a lifeboat and the next thing I knew I was washed up on a beach.
 I was on a desert island. I thought I was dreaming because it was so beautiful, but then the cold truth dawned on me - I was alone! I searched for the crew but all I found was one body so mangled I was sick.
 There were strange sights, smells and noises. I sat for a while but it started to get dark. I thought I had better make a shelter. I noticed a sail and some timber washed ashore, so I made a shelter.
 By this time I was desperate for the toilet so I dug a hole a short distance from my camp, and this was where I saw my first gorilla. It ran away. I went back to my camp. I sat looking out to sea. The sunset was beautiful, it took my breath away. Red, orange, green, the water shimmered like glitter. The stars and moon looked spectacular, then I slipped into a deep sleep and I dreamt of my family!

Clare Rowley (13)
Estover Community College, Plymouth

Untitled

Dear Diary,

I was on a journey to Spain to play in the football world tournament.

The England football team manager booked us a passage on his yacht HMS Sydney. It was a big luxury yacht with good living conditions.

I was looking forward to my journey and I was very excited. It was like a working holiday. All the team were happy.

We set off at sunset and the day looked promising, however as we journeyed on we noticed the wind had risen and the sea was choppy.

Day 2

Everything happened suddenly, the wind was howling and the sea beat fiercely against the yacht, it was frightening. The team and I were thrown overboard when the yacht capsized as it hit a sandy bay stuck out at sea. I managed to find a life craft and climbed over.

Day 3

After a while I found a palm tree island. I must have floated there when my life craft landed. Although I was alone I felt relieved that I was alive. I knew that all of my friends did not survive when the yacht was lost in the explosion as it hit the sandy bay.

Day 4

The island was deserted and peaceful, but I had to be sure there were no dangerous animals such as snakes, scorpions and spiders. There were many palm trees with dates and pineapples, also coconuts.

Day 5

After I recovered I looked for shelter and food. I thought maybe I could find something.

Daniel Wade (12)
Estover Community College, Plymouth

My Diary Of The Shipwreck

Dear Diary,
 I was on my way to Australia on the Brittany Ferries and I was enjoying my journey. They had lovely cabins and a pool outside. I went swimming all the time.
 I had just got in the pool when the fire alarm went off. The engine had caught on fire. I was really scared. The ship started to flood and I jumped into the sea.
 I swam to this island and just watched the ship sink underwater. The island looked peaceful. It had lots of trees which looked quite scary because they looked like the shadows of other people.
 I collected lots of fruit like pineapples and coconuts and built a fire to keep warm, but I was scared because it was getting dark. I saw a hut and there was a blanket so I slept in there overnight.
 In the morning I went outside. It was really hot. I went in the sea for a wash and to cool down.
 Then I saw a helicopter so I waved but they didn't see me. I was nearly crying but I didn't. I went for a swim in the sea but then I saw a shark's fin. I screamed and ran out of the water because it was chasing me.
 As the sun was setting, I heard a helicopter again. They saw me this time. When I got in the helicopter I saw my friend. I thought she was dead. I was really happy.

Sasha Holden (12)
Estover Community College, Plymouth

Red Arrow

David Bulpett is a Red Arrow pilot. He is the youngest Red Arrow pilot ever at the age of 21. Since he was 12 he'd dreamt of being a Red Arrow pilot.

Today is his first ever display flight and he is very nervous but excited. All his family are coming to the show. He has trained very hard for this day, he does not want to let his team down.

The day was as normal except for one bit that went wrong, when two planes collided and went spinning in all directions. The pilots ejected and landed safely.

Emergency help was ready and waiting, but the pilots were unharmed, the emergency men took the pilots to be checked over. The two planes exploded with a huge bang.

David Bulpett (12)
Estover Community College, Plymouth

Dear Diary

Dear Diary,
I was on my way to the Caribbean. I'd been there before. Last time on the ship it was sunny, this time it was raining. I was counting the days and I was very bored.

I was on the best ship. It had got a swimming pool and a steam room. I'd only had a chance to go in the pool. I was warm. I was looking forward to getting there because I'd see lots of wildlife and plants. I couldn't wait to go surfing, big waves, I couldn't wait!

I don't know what caused the shipwreck. I think it was a large rock, but it split the boat down the side. It is a state, a disaster. When it happened I felt very sad. I feel bad for the lives that have gone.

I climbed on top of the mast, dived into the water, then I couldn't remember any more after that. I didn't swim to the island, I just found myself there. It was very weird. I was freaked out. I felt great but still sad at the same time. I didn't know how long I was going to be there.

The island was very tropical, it had lots of animals and lots of different coloured plants.

I went looking round the island when I'd recovered to see if I could find anything useful.

When the sun went down, I felt glad because I had sunburn. My body was hurting and I needed a good night's sleep.

Sam Wooldridge (13)
Estover Community College, Plymouth

Crazy Colin Causes Crash

Yesterday there was a bad car crash in Blunts Lane, Estover. A young man, Harry Potter, 18, was knocked off his motorbike and died when his head hit the road.

Gary and Zoe Brown were driving a black Renault Megan and saw the crash happen. They called 999 and the police and an ambulance arrived soon after.

Harry was pronounced dead by the ambulance crew and his body was taken away to Derriford Hospital. The crazy driver who had caused the crash by speeding while talking on his mobile phone was questioned by police.

He was then taken to Derriford Hospital where his injuries were stitched. He remains in hospital and will be taken to Cranhill Police Station later.

Alex Lang (13)
Estover Community College, Plymouth

The Race

I was at a race with my dad, it was the best line up I had ever seen, but my dad never told me that my uncle was racing and he was going to take me in the car.

When my dad told me I was gobsmacked. He took me round to where my uncle's car was. It was the nicest car I had ever seen in my life. The car was blue and green. It was a BMW.

My uncle put me in the car and he said to me, 'Are you ready?' and off we went to the starting line.

The car was making a loud noise and the light was on red, then yellow, then green and off we went. We gradually went towards the front. It was 25 laps on the track.

The car stopped and smoke started to come out of the bonnet and all of the people started to run over the car.

The next thing I knew I was getting pulled out of the car window and a man was shouting at us to run. My uncle was still in the car.

At the end of the race my uncle came up to me and said he was sorry.

Phillip Marshall (13)
Estover Community College, Plymouth

Rob Had A Party

Rob had a party at the Jolly Miller, it was for his birthday and they all got very merry. Then Rob and his mates started to think about when they were younger. Rob's mate threw a glass at someone and started a fight, then it turned into a riot. Someone else pulled out a knife and stabbed Rob's mate. Rob called an ambulance but it was too late, his friend died in the Jolly Miller.

At 12am, the paramedics put him in the ambulance and took him to the hospital. The police arrived and started asking bags of questions. The police found the knife and took it back for fingerprints. Rob's mate, Tim, was only 20 years old, had everything to live for and in minutes he was dead.

As the week went by the police built their case when it finally went to court the man was found guilty of manslaughter and was given a five year prison sentence, but we will never see Tim again.

John Drake (15)
Estover Community College, Plymouth

The Wave - Which One Survived?
(Based on a true story)

December 20th 2004
    'Hello Frank, this is Dane. I am going to get married.'
    'That is amazing,' said Frank. 'When is the wedding?'
    'Christmas Day. It is in the Maldives.'
    'When are you coming back?'
    'On the 4th of January.'

December 21st 2004
    'Are we catching a train to Gatwick airport?'
    'Which airline?' asked Rachel.
    'Virgin Atlantic,' I said.
    'Better check in then.'
    We got on the jumbo jet, after that we went upstairs for our seats. We were in first class.
    Then the pilot spoke, 'We will be flying at 35,000 feet today and travelling at 500mph. We are taking off.'
    We landed in the Maldives early in the morning. The date was the 22nd December and the time was 2.30am. We went to our hotel on the seafront and went to sleep. We woke up in the late afternoon.

December 26th 2004
    The wedding was called off yesterday because the vicar was not well. Anyway the wedding is today, Boxing Day 2004. Also I had a good stag night.
    We drove down to the wedding in a limo. I sat down on a seat waiting for the bride to come. She looked beautiful. The vicar started and about 10 minutes later we were married. Everything was fantastic. 50 seconds later I saw a massive wall of water coming towards us. We had no chance. Goodbye Rachel.

Daniel Harvey (14)
Estover Community College, Plymouth

Mishka

Good morning, my name is Mishka. I am 3 years old. I am from Russia and I am a Russian blue. Today is a *purr*fect day with sunny spells all day, with light winds and the temperature is 20°C. What a glorious day it will be!

I have a family with 4 people in my house. The 2 older ones (the man and the woman) are in charge of the house, but they allow me to do anything that I want.

They are a lot better than my old family. My old family would pick me up in an unpleasant manner, chuck me in a polythene bag and swing it around with me in it. It was frightening.

After 6 months of nightmares they dumped me in the garbage bag to rot at the age of 1 year old. I just couldn't hack it, and now, 2 years later, here I am in a better life until a girl in my family keeps picking me up for a cuddle. I scratch and bite her until she lets me go.

My favourite country to go to is Turkey. It is a land with other cats like me, plus somewhere in the sun.

To be a cat you have to know the lifestyle, for example, we cats love to lick ourselves. Also, during the morning we have to watch the traffic - it can take hours to learn how to do it right.

Lawrence Bassett (14)
Estover Community College, Plymouth

When The Ship Goes Bang

Dear Diary,
 I was on my way to Corfu, sailing on the Mediterranean Sea where I was going to work for a week. I was on a huge cruise liner and it was a beautiful day. The sun was shining and the water was sparkling. I was looking forward to visiting Corfu because I'd never been before and had heard so much about it.
 We were nearly halfway when we saw two planes flying towards us, we didn't worry at first as we thought they were British planes. It wasn't long until we realised they were German planes about to bomb us. I was feeling scared at the time so I decided to jump off the ship before one of the bombs hit us.
 As I swam away as fast as I could, a large part of the cruiser landed on my head. It felt like it was a metal pole. It knocked me out cold.
 The next thing I knew I woke up on a beach. I didn't know where I was. I suddenly felt scared, there was no one around and no one to talk to. As I looked around I saw wild animals. There was a treehouse so I climbed up and looked around. I assumed someone had been there before as I saw lots of rotten food. As I turned around I saw that someone had died as there was a body in the treehouse. I walked around the corner and saw a beach.

David Carron (13)
Estover Community College, Plymouth

A Day In The Life Of A Lion

Hi, my name is Terry. I live in South Africa. With my flowing mane I am one of the most unmistakable sights on the African plains.

I live in a pride with 7 females and 13 cubs who are so annoying. The reason why you never see me hunting is because I am too big and it is difficult for me to hunt, and my mane gives me away.

Most people think we only hunt at night because it is cool and dark, but sometimes we hunt in the middle of the day because the rest of the animals are drinking or asleep.

The reason why I have a mane is because when I am fighting with other lions it protects my neck.

My roar can be heard from 5 miles away, impressive isn't it? We are the only big cats that live in a group.

Kayleigh Clarke (13)
Estover Community College, Plymouth

The Terrific Flood

14th March, 2pm. It was the time that rush hour began, life was all good until a random lorry came storming down the M5 at 90 miles per hour. 10 minutes later the random lorry came and crashed because of the speed the driver was driving at.

As the traffic started to build up, the boiling sun was heating up everyone in their cars.

Finally, after 3 hours, everybody was getting annoyed and fed up 'cause of the waiting. The person who was driving the lorry called the police and found out the problem. The problem was that there was oil pouring out of the back of the lorry. The police decided to clear the mess up.

8 hours later everyone was happy because they were getting through the traffic.

After that life was back to normal.

Charlotte Clarke (14)
Estover Community College, Plymouth

Dear Diary

Dear Diary,

I was on my way to Rome, Italy, to watch a football game, Rome Vs AC Milan. I was travelling on a luxury cruise boat and looking forward to the game.

I was playing football with my Beckham Shootout when I saw a rock in front of me. I ran to the wheel and tried to steer the boat but it did not have enough power to avoid the rock. I was upset. I can remember one more thing, all I could see was the floor beneath me starting to cave in.

The next thing I remember was waves crashing against my face. I woke up to find myself on a deserted island! I felt ecstatic to be alive and safe, but then I realised I was alone with no sign of the boat.

I was walking around the island to see if there was any more life but I could not find anything but coconuts. The island was lovely, it was full of trees and beaches. Most of my days were spent trying to build a raft to get me off the island but materials were scarce, so I had to improvise by using old ropes that had been washed in by the tide and old bits of driftwood. Also, I had to find a way to feed myself to keep up my strength.

As the sun started to go down I thought about my friends and family. I was so lonely and fed up with my own company.

Benjamin Mitchell (12)
Estover Community College, Plymouth

A Day In The Life Of Bob Burnquest

I was dreaming that I was Bob Burnquest and I had just skated through the corkscrew. All of my fans were there cheering me on. After this I was signing an autograph. When I finished signing it I was shot in the chest.

Four hours later I woke up but found myself in a hospital bed. I was allowed out three days later. I was unable to skate so I put all my money on a horse and it lost. I was stunned. I got a job in McDonald's. I went back into hospital to get the bullet removed.

Twelve hours later I woke up and found myself in my bedroom.

Chris Miles (14)
Estover Community College, Plymouth

Holiday From Hell

'Mum, Dad, I am really excited about tomorrow. I can't sleep at all.'

Mum said, 'You have to go to sleep or you will not get up to get the plane. *Now go to bed!*'

'Jordan, get up. It's time to go on holiday,' said Dad.

'What time is it please?' asked Jordan.

Dad said, 'It's 3.30.'

They got ready and went to the airport. As they went to get on the aeroplane their plane got delayed. Jordan was so excited, he could not wait to get on the plane. Then their plane was called out. Jordan ran onto the plane and sat down, but he could not sit still because he was so excited.

They landed at Disney Land. Jordan did not want to go to the hotel, he wanted to go on the rides. Jordan went on a roller coaster. As it looped, it stopped and they all fell out of their seats. They all went to hospital to get checked out. All Jordan had was a broken arm.

They got back to the hotel as they checked into their room Jordan walked into his room and saw someone dead on his bedroom floor …

Abby Cocking (14)
Estover Community College, Plymouth

Rob The Robot's Journey

One day on Planet Robo there was a robot called Rob the Robot and he was the hero of Planet Robo. But he had an evil brother called Bullet the Robot. He had an evil robot army and all his life he had tried to kill his bro. Bullet built an evil flying battleship called Bullet Blaster and he destroyed most of the planet.

Rob knew he needed to save the day again, but this was his toughest challenge yet. He went to the beach to talk to his best friend called Marco, but an evil robot shark called Sharmy ate him. Rob wanted revenge, he went to the bug bomb shop to buy some bombs. The bombs look like bugs because they have six legs. Rob threw eight bombs at the evil shark and he blew up. Rob saw a control battery on the broken shark; Bullet was controlling it. Rob wanted more revenge. He saw the oncoming battleship so he got a rocket from his bag and started to shoot at the battleship.

On the battleship there were guns everywhere and evil robots. Rob used a visibility battery so he went invisible and sneaked past all of them. He went to Bullet's battle area and fought him. They were shooting rockets, bullets and many more things. They were shooting for hours but Rob pushed him and Bullet was knocked out. Rob placed a bomb and jumped out of the battleship. The ship exploded but Rob got out at the last second.

Once again Rob saved the day!

Robert Crispin (14)
Estover Community College, Plymouth

Attacking Spiders
(Inspired by the film 'Eight x Legged Freaks')

One day there was a man who kept lots and lots of spiders and the man kept giving them water from the lake that he lives next to.

A couple of weeks later the spiders grew to about 8 foot.

The next day all of the spiders escaped from the man's house. There were jumping spiders and everything. The spiders started to kill people, but when they tried to kill the spiders, they took a long time to die.

The people agreed to blow up the family mall so they had to make sure that all of the spiders were inside the mall.

The next day they did it and the spiders died.

Luke Nicol (14)
Estover Community College, Plymouth

The Cellar

The cellar was a dark, dusty, cobwebby and damp place, but what lurked about inside was the scariest thing and the darkest, most dismal being you have ever seen, and possibly the most intelligent being you have ever seen. It had invented everything and placed it for other inventors to find and invent.

Nobody had ever seen the being before, he just moved stuff around like a poltergeist.

Then a family moved in called the Belimics. They were thugs, the whole lot of them. About 3 weeks after they'd moved in, Ben Belimic started to hassle this kid called Dave after he pushed Ben's mate Matt down a corridor and it all started from there.

After being chased, taunted and bullied in and out of school, Dave had had enough. He went to his mate who had contacts with the supernatural but he couldn't see the being. However, the being said he'd sort them out.

That night things started to go wrong for the Belimics. The being had got to work, he raised hell in that house and wrote a bloody message on the wall saying, 'Leave, leave, leave or you will die'.

The Belimics took the hint and left and never came back much to the delight of Dave.

David Gardener (14)
Estover Community College, Plymouth

Cover Blown

Matt, Dan and Jack were members of an elite police squad. Their mission was to recover the Crown jewels and capture the thieves who daringly stole them from the Tower of London. After weeks of careful planning and gathering of information, Dan had managed to gain their confidence and infiltrate the gang.

A week later, Matt and Jack received a phone call from Dan who was by then accepted and trusted by the thieves. He told them that the Crown jewels were being shipped over to Paris at 1pm that day. Dan gave them details of the route so they could intercept them before the precious cargo could be smuggled out of the country.

Dan returned to the hideout in an old derelict warehouse by the river. He'd been recruited to replace their driver after he had suddenly been taken ill. The jewels were about to be loaded into the van and Dan was going to meet the leader of the gang for the first time. Suddenly the phone rang ...

Plans had been changed, everything was in uproar. The schedule had been brought forward, they had to move fast. Seconds later, a black BMW screeched to a halt in front of the warehouse. Dan sneaked away to phone the squad to warn them. As he was about to speak he sensed someone behind him. Slowly he turned around, his blood ran cold and the phone slipped from his grasp. The line went dead!

Michael Davies (14)
Estover Community College, Plymouth

The Secret Treasure
(An extract)

'There it is,' exclaimed Jak as we flicked through the pictures of ancient Egyptian artefacts.

On the screen there was a gold figure shaped like a cat. Jak had been searching for this ancient figure for a few weeks.

A few hours before Jak had received the text; a golden figure had been stolen from a top French museum. Jak had received the text message from an anonymous sender and his number was withheld.

The message read, 'Jo, meet me at the docks on Friday evening, the figure is here and I am ready to make a lot of money.'

At the time Jak didn't understand the text but later on he worked out what was going on and phoned me up and told me what he knew. I was surprised but a bit curious and I wanted to follow the story up.

On Friday me and Jak cycled down to the docks and waited there for half an hour. We were hiding in a bush when a car pulled up next to a huge container ship. As it approached, two men got off the boat with a box in their hands. They were walking towards our bush when someone shouted from the boat behind.

'Help!'

The men placed the box on the ground and ran back onto the boat. I turned around to look at Jak as he pushed past me and picked up the box. As he picked it up, the man came out of his boat. Jak stood there frozen to the spot. He had two million pounds worth of artefact in his hands.

Troy Hill (14)
Estover Community College, Plymouth

Happy Slap

A young 14-year-old girl from Estover Community College, Plymouth is now in intensive care and rehabilitation unit after being attacked in what people are calling a 'Happy Slapping' incident.

Young Charlotte Marley was followed home by three girls in her year at school after getting off her usual bus at around 3.30pm on Monday 23rd June. After turning into a short cut through an alleyway the three girls ran towards Charlotte and forced her to the ground, they then kicked her, punched her and even stabbed her to a bloody pulp. The three girls then ran away, leaving Charlotte unconscious on the floor in the middle of an alleyway. Charlotte was found by Mr Williams who was walking past the alleyway around five minutes after the attack.

'The doctors said she was lucky I found her then', explained Mr Wiliams.

Luckily Charlotte is now in a stable state and is on the road to recovery. Charlotte's mum and dad are furious and are suing the three girls and their families for grievous bodily harm. The trial will be held later this week and all three defendants are pleading not guilty, even though a woman saw three girls running away from that area around 3.35pm on Monday 23rd June. Let's hope they don't get off easily!

Michael Raven (14)
Estover Community College, Plymouth

A Day In The Life Of José Antoni Reyes
(An extract)

As I arrived at José's house, him and his girlfriend greeted me at the entrance to his mansion in the suburbs of London. Although it was a match day and Arsenal were playing Chelsea at 3pm, José still had time to talk to me about his daily routine. I thought this was very good of him considering the long day ahead.

As it neared lunchtime José showed me his magnificent house and his awesome collection of cars. Around 12.30, José and his partner packed the car ready for the 40 minute trip to the hotel where the rest of the Arsenal squad were to meet.

As we left his home, José told me how it had been hard to settle in at Arsenal, but how his Spanish friend Cesc Fabregas helped him and how they relied on each other for help to settle in.

When we arrived at the hotel, his teammate Robin van Persie came over and spoke to José about the job ahead and how him and José would be the main part of Arsenal's striking partnership as Thierry Henry was out with a calf injury.

When we arrived at Highbury, spirits were high and José spoke with the great confidence that had spread after the win over Charlton in mid week.

Corey Marshall (14)
Estover Community College, Plymouth

A Day In The Life Of A Treasure Hunter

I awoke on a nervous stomach. Today felt like the day I was going to find The Charlotte. As we set off on our journey through the snow on our snow mobiles, I suddenly felt like I was really close to something so I ordered my friend Giles to immediately stop. I had a strange feeling at the bottom of my stomach. We got out the metal detectors and began our search. It felt like hours but then, *beep, beep, beep*, the metal detector went off. I got down in the snow and immediately started digging. All of a sudden there it was, she was beautiful, I had to get inside her.

As we walked through there were loads of barrels full of gunpowder but there was a certain barrel which the captain was protecting. There had to be something good in it so I looked and there it was, the next clue. I had been waiting all my life to find the next clue but now I'd found it, it didn't feel real. With the clue came a riddle. I started to read it out loud. After a while of going over it in my head I had clocked it, but as I started to tell the answer to the riddle, my so-called friend Giles pulled out his gun on me and tried to kill me to get the treasure for himself but I wasn't going to let that happen.

Jessica Loomes (14)
Estover Community College, Plymouth

A Day In The Life Of Dolly The Dog

'Miaow, hiss.'
'Snore ... !'
'Shut up!'
That's what I'd hear every morning, the cats fighting and crying, my owners snoring. Can't a dog get any sleep!

In the morning I would wait until both my owners get up, then I would plod downstairs to have some food. Well, that's if the cats hadn't stolen it, they usually did. Then I would sit by the back door, ears pricked up, waiting so that I could have a pee, sometimes my owners would just look at me, I mean - *open the door!*

By noon, after having my nap, I would find one of my cuddly toys and keep it in my mouth until one of my owners would take it, then throw it so I would chase it, I would have lots of fun. Anyway, in five minutes I would be exhausted and if it was sunny, I would go outside and sleep, otherwise inside.

When my owners' daughter arrived home, I would run to the door barking loud, pleased to see her, hoping to receive a treat or two and a cuddle. After teatime I would rather sleep, so I would crawl into the nearest basket and doze, occasionally peering around to see what was happening. Then I would sleep again.

If you haven't guessed, I'm not alive anymore but that was my life, a day in the life of Dolly (me) the dog.

Amelia Downing (15)
Estover Community College, Plymouth

The Sun

Footballer Attacked

Soccer ace, Thierry Henry, was brutally attacked by a group of Chelsea supporters. They were said to have followed him to his home near London and smashed open Thierry's door. They smashed him across the head twice with a steel bar and hit him across his ribs with a golf club. Luckily his friend and teammate, Robert Pires, drove over to Thierry's mansion in his Porche 911 turbo and he scared away the Chelsea fans. Thierry Henry will miss two friendlies against Poland and Brazil in the first three games of the new season. His injuries are three cracked ribs, a broken cheekbone and slight signs of whiplash and concussion. Thierry's boss called the attackers, 'brutal and savage people who should get locked up'. The makers of the wristbands have come up with a black and yellow wristband saying 'Beat Hooligans'. Thierry has put up a £15,000 reward to the person who gives evidence to the police that leads to the prosecution of these brutal attackers.

Daniel Loveless (14)
Estover Community College, Plymouth

A Day In The Life Of Daniel Brown

19th July 2005 - 8.30am

Dear Diary,
　　I'm so excited about the match! It's going to be class! A Man United scout is coming to watch me! I just can't wait! Kick-off's not till 3pm so I've got ages to wait. My life would be perfect if Man United win the Champions League, Plymouth Tigers (my team!) win the double (cup and league) and I get picked to play for Manchester United U14s! I've been working towards this since I was 9, that's 4 years! Mum keeps telling me not to get my hopes up. If Dad could see me now he'd be so proud. He died in a car crash 2 years ago.
　　Anyway, my favourite team, Man United (of course), have got into the final of the Champions League and they're up against AC Milan! But I better get ready now, it's 9am and I have to be at the stadium for 1pm. I've got to go food shopping with Mum as well! I'll write later, tell you how it went! Wish me luck!
　　Dan.

7pm

Dear Diary,
　　Just got home! Plymouth Tigers absolutely thrashed Torquay Owls, 6-2! Man United beat AC Milan on penalties (5-4)! and the best part of it all is we're moving up to Manchester so I can play for them! We've got a house up there, well we have now that the others have pulled out! Well I probably won't write in this diary again because I'll be too busy! So farewell forever, I suppose!
　　Dan.

Charlotte Nicholson (14)
Estover Community College, Plymouth

I Remember

Silence.

A great sheet of quietness covered over the cubical as the nurses pulled over the sheet which covered up my frail grandfather's face.

His last words were, 'Live your life in which I lived mine'. I wasn't quite sure what he meant, but he gazed at me, as if to say goodbye.

The rain kept on falling. I kept on thinking that I would see him walking around the corner in the shops or something, but the only thing I had left of him was his army badges. I've always liked them, ever since I was little. My grandad used to let me wear them every time I saw him. I used to pretend I was an army officer and prance around, telling everyone what to do.

I loved my grandad. I listened to his every word. He would tell me the most exciting stories and give the best advice. Everyone was so proud of the way he used to look after us all and I still wish he was here to look after me.

To me this seems a little bit strange, but sometimes I can hear him talking to me and sometimes I talk back to him.

It has been a few weeks now since my grandad passed away and I can't stop thinking about him. The other day my gran told me I should move on.

Bang!

I sat upright in my bed and there he was. After dreaming and hoping he would come back. Was it a dream?

Megan Chamberlaine (14)
Estover Community College, Plymouth

And There I Was

Bang!

And there I was, just standing there. Shocked, I stood still and, from that moment in time, my world fell apart.

I gazed down like an eagle in the midnight sky and there he was, just lying there, helplessly, as a tear fell from his eye. He then breathed his last breath and one last time closed his eyes. A shuffle of the rubble beneath me ended the silence. I ran from the scene, it wasn't meant to be this way.

It was an accident!

Many days passed until his body was found. Everyone was crying at school but me. No, the only emotion I felt was guilt. 3 days later the murder enquiry started, the worst days of my life, each day my guilt grew worse. What was I to do? What was the right thing? What questions would they ask me? Many days passed before they came for me. They apologised for hassling me at such a harsh time. They said things like, 'Where were you on the night of Michael's death?' and, 'You must be devastated on the news of your dear friend's death'.

They said he was my friend, yes, my friend. It rang over in my head like an unanswered telephone. Me and Michael were enemies. I meant to shock him but instead I drove him to death.

10 years later.

Happily married with 3 precious children. I'm 26 now. Each day the guilt stands over me. They never found me guilty, yet shadows of the night remain my deepest fear.

Nicola Taylor (14)
Estover Community College, Plymouth

The Times

Teen Pregnancy

Over the past few years, teenage pregnancies have become a problem, they have been rising by the minute, but is this the children's fault? No, it's the parents', they haven't been teaching them any morals. They have no respect for themselves, they can't seem to say no.

One family in Dorset, consisting of a mother and three daughters, aged 16, 14 and 12 have just appeared on the documentary program on ITV 1, 'Tonight With Trevor McDonald'. The subject was 'Teenage Pregnancies', all three of the children had become pregnant with their mother's consent. Not only is this illegal, it is morally wrong and should be widely discussed in schools all over the world.

So, the question is, why are they like this?

As I said before, the parents and carers aren't teaching them that it is perfectly acceptable to say no and the media doesn't help. Recently, on 'EastEnders', a young girl, about 14, has just had a baby and they didn't make much of it, everything looked very pleasant and easy, but they have got to realise that it isn't, it's not like a doll, you just dress it and make it look pretty, having a child is very hard work, and they don't stay babies forever, they grow up.

What can we do to prevent this from happening? First of all we can set up workshops all over the country showing all of the children how hard it is bringing up a child and how when you're so young that it can wreck your life, and that having a baby would prevent them from doing what they want to do when they get older.

Erin Horrell (13)
Estover Community College, Plymouth

A Day In The Life Of Me

Today is my stepsister Aimee's birthday. Yet again we have all been forgotten and Aimee is the centre of attention - no change there then. Skye, my real sister, and I are totally invisible to Dad and everyone else in the house. We are just about to leave for the beach where Aimee is hosting the party of the year - not! She has invited practically her whole year, even people she doesn't know! And now I am forced to spend a perfectly good Saturday bored out of my brains watching Queen Aimee get everything she could ever need and more! Fair enough, it's her birthday, but it's not just now it's all the time. Aimee, Aimee, Aimee, 24/7. I just wish Dad would have time for me. I expect I will write again later, that is if I don't get caught up in all the excitement!

I told you I'd be back, but with some good news this time. We were all waiting to go home to have a barbecue when suddenly we heard a noise come from the rock pools. It sounded like Aimee screaming. We ran to see if she was OK. When we got there she had been bitten by a crab. Everyone was in fits of laughter. She was so distraught she sent everyone home and vowed never to leave the house again! It was the best day of my life, well, until another of Aimee's parties anyway!

Zoe Roberts (13)
Estover Community College, Plymouth

My Final Breaths

Bang! I shot upright from my bed. Darkness covered me like a blanket. *Bang!* It came again. Finally I plucked up the courage to go downstairs. Slowly I crept down and there it was again. *Bang!* Although this time I realised it was coming from outside. Then, as I opened the door, I heard the roar of a classic and the sound of tyres wheel-spinning on the ground.

I decided to investigate. I slipped on my trainers and went outside into the bitter cold in just my pyjamas. I was determined to find out what that sound was. I checked every house, nothing seemed suspicious. I felt every engine, none were warm. Then I came to *his* house. The one whose name is never mentioned. The gate to his eerie mansion was open and his Bentley's engine was warm.

I crept round the back undetected. Strangely, the basement door was open so I snuck in. I found myself in a crowded library and I fell over a chair leg and onto a bookcase. A secret door opened, so I ran behind a pile of books.

He shouted out, 'Who's there?'

I heard him stomping closer and closer. My heart missed a beat. I peered through a gap and saw he had my mum's head in his hand. For some strange reason he had a pitchfork in the corner. I grabbed it and thrust it into his chest. He dropped to the floor. Then I committed suicide.

Dan Tucker (14)
Estover Community College, Plymouth

Murder In Doomville

On November 14th, 1974 police received a frantic phone call leading them to a grisly investigation at the Yeswits' residence in Doomville. An entire family had been slaughtered in their beds. The Yeswits' son confessed to the shooting of his parents and four siblings (5-16) while they slept. He said 'the voices' in the house lead him to the killing. When they went to investigate, they only found four bodies not six.

One year later George and Katie Luctus moved in with three children. They thought it was a wonderful home until strange goings on began to happen. One time Father Hagins came to free the evil presence from the house and saw Katy's daughter Shannon had a teddy bear which apparently was left behind but Father Hagins said it was buried with the Yeswits' daughter.

Another incident where Shannon somehow got onto the roof of the house and was shouting to her mother, she was frightened that Shannon would fall so she rushed into the room and climbed up the gutter and asked Shannon what she was doing. Now Shannon had lost her dad, George was her stepdad. She said Zoey wanted to show her her dad and stepped off the edge. Katy grabbed her in time and tried to get a grip, the sleeve began to rip! Shannon fell, George caught her.

Things got unbearable and 28 days later they left the house forgetting everything that had happened, luckily escaping with their lives.

Sophie Seldon (12)
Estover Community College, Plymouth

My First Try

It was the 13th October 2003 and the team were going to their first set of rugby matches. It was our first chance to try out what we'd learnt in training. We were really nervous because we did not know what to expect. As we got onto the bus, everyone had mixed feelings of nerves and excitement. As we set off the weather was fine, with a few black clouds in the sky. Everyone was really chatty on the bus, talking about how nervous or excited they were. More than half were talking about hoping to score a try.

We were all hoping to be included in the match. Then I found out that I was going to play. We were focused from the beginning to the end. As the game commenced backs and forwards alike were ready. As much as everyone tried they could not break the 0-0 deadlock, until Estover suddenly made a break. Alex McGraw, (one of the second rows) missed the pass because he tripped. That trip gave us the lead though, because he knocked somebody out of the way. This gave me, Chris Brooking, the inside centre of the squad, a chance to grab the ball and dive for the line. When I dived I felt as if I was in slow motion, I took a blow to my jaw and then I realised I'd got over the line and scored. Eventually Estover won 15-5. We were over the moon.

Christopher Brooking (13)
Estover Community College, Plymouth

George And Pink, Will It Catch On?

This morning as people from all over the world woke, they knew nothing of the day ahead.

Last night, after having a private interview with Pink, George Bush dramatically changed his hairstyle from home dyed brown to *pink!* But does the nation approve?

As shops opened at 8.30am Americans from all over the world raided them. Any normal person would think World War III was about to start. *Pink* was now the new black. Questions from all over the world will be asked, why? Why pink?

Has the nation had a revolution? George Bush said, 'After speaking to Pink last night I realised just how much pink affected our world. The pink make-up, the pink flowers in the spring ...'

After running over the tapes made this morning we realised that every sentence said by Bush included the word 'pink'. So how will this affect the world? That's the outcome we'd all like to see.

But what about goths? Will they turn pink or will black stay their black?

Jessica Veacock (12)
Estover Community College, Plymouth

A Day In The Life Of A Soldier

Dear Diary,
   Two weeks into the Second World War and bombs are still dropping like rain. I haven't heard silence since it started. Already people are dead or injured. I feel terrified. But I will fight. I will do justice for my country.
   Me and my best friend, James Barron, are still alive and sticking together. He is on the other side fighting at the moment. I, however, have ducked behind a large hill writing, petrified of going out, putting all my feelings down on a piece of paper.
   Oh no! There has just been a very big explosion on the other side of the camp. People are screaming ... Another explosion has gone off. More soldiers are running, blood pouring down their faces. Their faces terrified; their eyes cannot believe what they have seen. Another explosion has gone off and more and more people are screaming. I see strong soldiers being carried to safety. It suddenly occurs to me ... James! We have known each other our whole lives, he couldn't be dead. I get up and start running to where the explosion has happened. I start shouting his name, but I can't hear anything; all I can hear is the sound of war. I can't see anything either. It is misty and pouring down with rain. Then suddenly I hear my name, 'Robert! Robert please help me!' It is James, I know it is.
   'Watch out! bomb!' I hear a soldier cry ...

Natasha Arnold (13)
Estover Community College, Plymouth

A Day In The Life Of My Guinea Pig Pumba

Hi, my name is Pumba I am a ginger, dark brown and white coloured guinea pig. I wake up every morning and squeak until I get food. I used to have a hutch mate called Timon but she died a few months back, as she had a sore chest. My owners and I miss her very much. I am not allowed another friend as Emma's parents say she isn't allowed.

I have a happy life and I get cuddled every day. Emma tries to talk to me but I don't understand what she is saying. When my owners go out to work and school I eat my food and play in my run, where I play 'hit' with the flies that fly around my hutch. I always win.

When my owners have a holiday the next-door neighbours, Janet or Joan, look after me. They take good care of me but I do miss Emma. When she comes back from holiday, I squeak so she hugs me but she is normally too busy running in and out of the house unpacking. So I waddle into the dark side of the hutch where I sleep, then Emma wakes me up to give me a nice warm hug and a kiss.

I enjoy Saturdays as my hutch has a nice clean. I get put in a special guinea pig box whilst Emma cleans my hutch, she doesn't enjoy it as I make it smell. I always look forward to coming back to a nice clean hutch.

Emma Humphries (13)
Estover Community College, Plymouth

The Creature

She crept cautiously into the room. Not knowing what was in there. She heard creepy noises coming from the darkness. What the noise was she didn't know? She thought it sounded like chains, rusty old chains. No, it was more of a moaning, groaning sound. Smoke forming on the floor. A growling sound filled the darkness.

A shape started to form in the distance. It was big and broad. It was strange-looking. She tried to switch on the light, to see the creature that stood before her. Nothing happened.

Drip, drop. The sound of dripping filled the room. Was it blood? Was it water? She didn't know. Then suddenly *bang!* The door shut behind her. Her body shaking with fear. Not being able to move. She was shocked with fear, for she didn't know what horrible creature stood before her.

The creature moved towards her. She could smell its rancid breath next to her cheek. The only thing she could hear was her racing heartbeat. When she tried to turn her head away the creature moved closer. Its warm drool dripping onto her face.

She reached out a trembling hand, and felt a solid wall of matted fur. She felt warm blood explode from her arm, as the creature's claws slashed through her flesh like a hot knife in butter.

This was it, she was gong to die. Just as all hope was lost, the light came on ...

Amy Mouncher (13)
Estover Community College, Plymouth

Set-Up

'*President gunned down in tragic drive-by*' scream the headlines and all the newspapers read something like: 'A man on the rampage robbed an ammunition store and later stole a motorbike from the local showroom. He then drove right through all roadblocks and gunned down the President who was giving a speech. Four bodyguards died protecting him. The rampaging madman then disappeared and has not been seen since'. But that's not what happened and I know, I shot them. The President is alive and well, he was not the target, his bodyguard was. The bodyguard was an assassin. He was being paid an immense sum of money to kill the President. It was all set up by the CIA. The security breach was carefully planned to make sure someone didn't assassinate the President for real. 'Why all this?' I hear you ask. I'll tell you what really happened from the beginning.

Yesterday, when I got home from PCFE, the CIA approached me and they asked me if I was interested in a trip to America. I agreed because they offered me £1,000,000,000 if I helped them. They wanted me to remove one of the President's bodyguards but make it look like the President was the target. This would be best accomplished by shooting the bunch of them with blanks but killing the assassin. They also explained why they'd chosen me. They'd chosen me because the people paying the assassin would recognise an agent. So here I stand ... a billionaire.

Marek Vincenc (13)
Estover Community College, Plymouth

Murdered

Joe Davies was late last night murdered by prison jail breaker Adam Park, Adam later said sorry, he thought Joe was going to stop him or tell on him to the police. Joe (16) was shot in the jaw twice and rushed to hospital about 7am. The serious injuries later left him to die sadly in pain. One day after death, Joe's mum said, 'What kind of sick person would do this? He was just going to a friend's house, didn't do any harm'. She also said, 'I hope he gets what's coming to him in prison and rots in h*ll'.

Joe was killed going through Asda Park Bristol, the Gorge blesses Joe and hopes he rests in peace, he will always be remembered by all. His sister also said he was the best brother in the world. His school coach said he was Mr Estover for basketball and top for football.

His friends from Estover will build a bench with a plaque on it for his remembrance. He will be buried on Tuesday 17th May at 12 midday. His tutor said, 'He was a very polite boy, and was very athletic. A one minute silence will be held for him by teammates from Plymouth Rangers and other teams on Saturday and he will be given 'Players' Player award'.

Steven France (14)
Estover Community College, Plymouth

Boat Trip

We left the harbour at four o'clock in the morning. The weather was calm, the other fishing boats were getting ready to go.

Three hours out to sea it was starting to get exciting when it began to rain the wind increased and the journey became very bumpy. We were fishing for two days, had a few bites. We travelled out into the Atlantic and saw some dolphins swimming towards us, suddenly a great shoal of fish were heading our way. There was a massive rumble and an enormous wave headed towards us, we were petrified. The captain decided to steer into the wave. At first the boat coped well but at a great speed we held our breath. In a state of shock and with the sound of creaking we lowered the dinghy without delay. I jumped overboard and there was not time to think. I was alone. Where were my brothers? I was very frightened. Fortunately I managed to drag myself over the side of the dinghy. After searching for what seemed like hours I fell asleep.

The rays of sun blinded me as I stirred from under my jacket which was sheltering me from the cold ...

Danny Kendall (13)
Estover Community College, Plymouth

Shely And The Beast

All of the place is covered in fireballs. There are trees. There is a river. There were mountains with snow on top. All over all of the mountains there were sleeping people and the villages were ruined.

The beast picked up all the people. It was snowing. She turned them into stone. Everyone was fed up with the beast. They decided to get the hero called Shely to help them.

Shely got red-eyed when she got angry and her eyes turned to lasers that could burn through the skin and bone. Lines on top of the mountain show where she had been. The beast was turning people to stone. Shely was sent for to help.

On her way she met a wizard who gave her wings and a magic potion to make her invisible. She found the beast and drank her magical potion. The beast couldn't see her so she used her laser eyes and blew the beast up.

Shely took all the little pieces to show the village people that the beast was dead. The people in the village were so very happy that Shely had killed the beast that they offered her anything. Shely had always loved the most handsome man who lived there so Shely and her man called Derek were married.

Georgia Ball (12)
Hillside Special School, Plymouth

The Queen, Bob The Beast And Phoenix

The beach as quiet, stony, salty and grey. The people had been turned to stone like statues. The sky was grey.

The horrible beast called Bob had turned nearly all the people to stone. He was very strong and could jump into the sky. The Queen asked Phoenix, the hero, to save them by burning the beast's eyes. Phoenix was also strong and powerful and he was the only one who could fight Bob. He could fly and burn people, so he went and looked for Bob, but didn't know where he was so couldn't find him. He got lost and asked people where the beast was, but they couldn't answer because they were stone. He turned a stone woman back to her original state by using a potion and she gave him a map. He didn't turn back all the stone people yet because the beast was still alive and it would be a waste of potion.

In the far distance, Bob was coming towards him. He had to think quickly. Suddenly, he decided to burn him right in the eyes. It hit him in the eyes. He fell to the ground and died.

Phoenix picked Bob off the ground and carried him to the Queen. On the way, he opened the bottle of powerful potion and used it to turn the stone people back to normal. They helped Phoenix carry Bob. In return for Bob's death, the Queen married Phoenix on the blue and golden sandy beach.

Darren Davis (13)
Hillside Special School, Plymouth
(Now attends Coombe Dean School)

Darren And Golum
(Golum inspired by 'The Hobbit' and 'The Lord of the Rings' trilogy by J R R Tolkein)

The cliff was high. Stones fell and as they fell they caught alight. It took each rock a year to fall. Skeletons lay down on the cliff chained to the wall. They were killed by Golum years ago. Golum stood at the top of the cliff in the darkness and whispered, 'My precious.'

The beast had short hair and large ears. He was greyish and his favourite saying was, 'My precious'. Wherever he went, he ate people alive. He chewed them and burnt them. He had killed thousands. The people needed Darren, the speed man, to save them.

Darren only took two seconds to get there because he wore the fastest shoes in the world and ran and ran and ran. When Darren and Golum saw each other, Golum curled up and said, 'Can I help you, my precious?' he licked his lips and led Darren to him by curling his finger. Darren did not fall for it but ran so quickly past that Golum's ear ripped off.

Darren picked up the bleeding ear, put it in a jar and carried it back to the people to show them that Golum had bled to death. The stones stopped falling and the people rewarded him by making him king of their land.

Craig Knight (12)
Hillside Special School, Plymouth

The Hero And The Beast

Down in the woods, the dark woods, a tree suddenly caught on fire. It collapsed. They ran as fast as they could.

The beast was scary. He had got eyes. He used his eyes. He burnt nearly everything.

The battle began. The hero got there in three days. He flew in three aeroplanes. When he got there, he saw the headmaster beast who said he needed help because he couldn't handle the little beast. There was burning the beast to do now. Then he gave the little beast a pair of scissors which exploded the him.

The hero put the dead little beast into his sack and carried him away from his dad. 'Bye bye, son. I hate you!'

'Let me go!'

'No!'

'Fine, kill me!'

'OK I will!'

He took him to the special machine and tried to kill him. Here, now! *Five, four, three, two, one, crash, bang, boom!* The hero laughed three times and turned the little beast into stone. He whacked him with a bat and he crunched him up into little pieces. The headmaster beast said, 'What on Earth is this?' But the hero got poorly and went to bed. After a few years, he was better but the headmaster beast had died and although the hero took him to hospital he didn't get better because he'd killed the little beast. The hero was made king of the world for saving everyone around the world from the burning beasts.

Gareth Lewis (13)
Hillside Special School, Plymouth

Mr Green And The Beast

On a very snowy mountain where people say that a big, white, furry, beastly monster lived and frightened or killed all the people that tried to climb his mountain there was a beast. The beast burnt the land and destroyed the crops and the people with his eyes. The beast kept burning everybody and melting them with his tail.

The hero swam to the beast to kill it. His reward was that he would marry the King's daughter. The hero picked up a large, shiny mirror outside and tied it to his back so he could swim. When Mr Green, the hero, got there he dropped a sack over the beast's head and when the beast took it off Mr Green shone the mirror at the beast so that his burning eyes burnt him inside.

Mr Green filled a pot with beast juice to take to the Queen to prove that the beast was dead. When he walked back to the snowy mountain, beast juice dripped onto the ground and, like Medusa's blood drips turned to stone, the beast juice drips turned into spiders with burning eyes. The hero didn't notice. When Mr Green gave the Queen the beast juice and everyone cheered, the Queen asked him to stay and live on the mountain. The snow melted and the sun came out.

Raymond Steyn (13)
Hillside Special School, Plymouth

Sharon And Gorgon Paul

The clouds were grey. Small and tall people had been turned to stone. There was long grass on tiny mountains. Smoke was flashing through the grass from the beast called Gorgon Paul. Everywhere people were looking around the mountains to make sure they saw Gorgon Paul before he saw them.

Gorgon Paul had tall, gross nails. He had snakes around his hair. His hair was blond and the snakes were blond and turned people into stone. They needed a hero. Sharon's mother was gong to be forced to marry the beast who was very ugly. Sharon's mother loved somebody else.

Sharon, the hero, flew to save her mother. She looked behind with her shiny shield and killed the beast. Her golden hair made her invisible so that she could find the beast. Sharon hid behind a rock. She cut off the beast's head and took it to show that she had won.

Sharon was rewarded with great riches for killing the beast and saving her mother because now her mother could marry the man she really wanted.

Nikita Wood (13)
Hillside Special School, Plymouth

Nemesis And Lenny

There was once a hero called Nemesis. Nemesis liked to wear a large suit with a big 'N' on the front of it. He also had some flying shoes.

Nemesis lived in the village Gran. Village Gran was a quiet village with no crime. There was a castle in the village where a mean and nasty beast lived.

Nemesis was given a staff by an old man. It could make thunder. It was a reward for saving three people. Lenny, Nemesis' brother decided he wanted to find and kill the beast as well.

The beast was blue with red streaming eyes. It could shoot its finger nails at people.

Whilst walking through tombstones the beast attacked Nemesis and tried to take his staff. Mummies poured out of the tombs and hurt Lenny. Nemesis waved his staff, though, and electrocuted the beast with lightning. The mummies ran away and he and Lenny were safe even though there was blood everywhere.

Steven Lilley (13)
Hillside Special School, Plymouth

Hurk And The Dragon

In Italy, near the seaside there was a boy called Hurk. He was strong, beautiful and big. What was his quest? He had to kill a fire-breathing dragon that had kidnapped his brother Jake.

He set off on his journey across the sea. It was so misty you couldn't see your hand in front of your face. The waves were crashing against his ship and the wind was blowing.

Someone told Hurk where the dragon was. He sneaked up into the cave and blew up the dragon with a stick of dynamite. Luckily he had freed his brother by creeping him past the dragon whilst it was asleep. Jake was scared but then happy when he saw Hurk.

Ryan Harvey (13)
Hillside Special School, Plymouth

Beast Slayer And The Ice Beast

A long time ago in Iceland there was once a man called Beast Slayer. He lived in the snowy mountains. It was very cold and icy there.

Beast Slayer went on a mission to kill an Ice Beast because it was eating people's cattle. He had a journey to the other side of the world to make. His journey was long and tiring. People helped Beast Slayer by giving him food and water.

Beast Slayer managed to find the Ice Beast near a volcano. He started to fight the monster. He kicked the Ice Beast who roared. *'Roar.'* The Ice Beast was kicked over onto hot ground and he melted. Beast Slayer went back to Iceland to celebrate with a party.

Daniel Smith (13)
Hillside Special School, Plymouth

Nemesis' Revenge!

Nemesis lived in Greenland in a castle. He was planning to kill a snow wolf which had killed his brother.

The snow wolf was black with brown splodges. Blood often dripped from his fangs.

Nemesis had a special Samurai sword to protect him. He went looking for the snow wolf in the icy mountains. The wolf was hiding in a frozen river; it jumped out on Nemesis who ran into the cold, damp caves.

Inside they fought and when Nemesis managed to kill the wolf he was surprised to find that it turned into his brother!

Adam Krisht (13)
Hillside Special School, Plymouth

Nemesis And The Electric Spam Killer

It started in an Asian jungle in the village of Catspee. Nemesis was strong, handsome, muscular and he is a beast slayer. He was after the ugliest monster of them all - the Electric Spam Killer!

The Electric Spam Killer had an electric collar because he was a robot.

Nemesis found the Electric Spam Killer in the jungle. Suddenly he saw his brother getting swallowed up by the monster. Nemesis went to stab the Spam Killer. He sliced open the beast and his brother fell out okay. Nemesis was happy to see his brother and his brother was pleased to be out and alive!

Jamie Hosking (12)
Hillside Special School, Plymouth

The Green Goblin And The Dartmoor Dust

It was a bitter cold night. The mist had drifted in from the red settled sunset. Nothing could be heard. There was a bright glowing moon.

Disguised by the mist, a huge deep wishing well was being opened. A dark droopy green goblin shot out of the wishing well. He had been waiting for forty years to come out.

The nearest town was just at the bottom of the tor. The angry green goblin struck at the Lord Mayor of Dartmoor's house. When the Lord Mayor answered the door, the angry green goblin committed murder using an axe to the throat. No one had found the Lord Mayor. The green goblin had found the keys to the creepy cellar where the Lord Mayor's grandfather had been haunting the stone crystal, but upstairs the light was twitching and flickering where the dark bull had been waiting for food and was very fierce.

The dark bull and the green goblin destroyed the town. The crystal helped destroy the town. The town turned into dust that floated across Dartmoor above the moon.

Lewis Joyce (13)
Hillside Special School, Plymouth

The Skeletons, The Priest And The Gloves

The sky was cloudy, stormy and dark. The moon was a half moon. There was a dark blue and black shadow around and under the moon. In the cemetery were gravestones. There were dead flowers and bones of skeletons between the graves. There were four skeletons laying down by the tree with no leaves on it. Thunder crashed and rain dripped and dripped onto the graves. Blood ran into the rainwater.

The skeletons had started to come out of the graves. The blood was there because they were dead. They started killing everybody and everybody was screaming and turning into skeletons. The skeletons came up from the trees. They had come alive and everyone was sitting down, and eating fresh blood and fresh bodies from the graves.

The children saw the skeletons and ran and screamed. A priest heard the children and ran to them. The priest saw the skeletons and rang for help. People from everywhere came, put gloves on and picked up the skeletons.

Sarah Symons (14)
Hillside Special School, Plymouth

Was It True?

In the woods, there was a sinking mist. It was wet and cold. It was thundering. Then there was silence. Children were crying. It was dark and shadows were moving nearer to them. They were shaking because they saw something that was scary. They ran away from it. There was a dead body. It was very scary.

The children went to the old woman's house. The woman rang for the ambulance. The ambulance doctors came and they told the old woman to tell the children it was fake. But the question still waits to be answered. Was it true?

Josieanne Thyer (14)
Hillside Special School, Plymouth

The Missing Man

One dark night at the graveyard there was a man who went out to the graveyard and did not come back. The weather was dry, misty, cloudy and dark. There was a full moon and the trees looked like faces.

In 1878, there was an inspector. He brought his friends with him to the creaky old graveyard in Deon. When the inspector and his friends got to the castle they booked a night inside. He was in bed until he heard a noise outside the window. He got out of his bed and went downstairs to see what it was. When he got outside, he saw something in the distance. He walked to see what it was until he ran into an old man. The inspector talked to the old man who said, 'Beware of the wolf. He can eat human flesh.'

So the inspector went after the wolf. When he saw it again it was not far away. He got his gun out and shot the wolf-dog dead on the top of the tor. He returned back to the castle to tell his friends that the Dartmoor curse was gone for good.

Thomas Channing (14)
Hillside Special School, Plymouth

The Ways Of Dartmoor

On a spooky night under a full moon there stood a haunted house with a graveyard right outside it. Inside the house were creaking floorboards and dangling spiders with eerie-looking eyes. Creaky sounds could be heard from all over the house. There were ghosts, bats and eerie looking windows which could make you scream.

Outside the haunted house was a graveyard. A shock of fright rushed around the misty air as dead bodies came alive laughing with a frightening laugh that could make you run. The bodies lurked in the shadows waiting for human blood. They needed the blood to stay alive. Wailing witches flew around and ghosts of Dartmoor started to haunt. Trees looked at you with their eyes.

Witches flew over villages and ghosts waited overhead. The trees lifted their roots and started walking around laughing, and with evil cackling laughs, terrified the villagers who fled their villages. But some villagers did not make it in time. A few survivors screamed for help, but it did not come quickly enough.

Rebecca Armitage (14)
Hillside Special School, Plymouth

The Hound Of The Dartmoor Tors

Under a full moon, the foggy weather drifted in-between the tors. You could hear the howling of the mysterious beast echoing and vibrating through the shadowy woods. Shadows which looked like faces from the trees stared at the man.

As it always does on Friday the thirteenth, when the full moon shines through the woods, the beast jumped out with claws and stabbed the man.

In the morning there were some people walking who found the body. They phoned some hunters. To find what had killed the man they went out to find the killer and found some little traces of blood and footprints, which looked like beast footprints.

The path of prints was leading them through the woods into a graveyard to where there was freshly turned soil on only one grave. So they lifted up the lid of the grave. There were bones like legs of chickens. Suddenly, the beast jumped out on one of the men and killed him. Another man shot the beast through the heart and killed it.

Now when they go out at night between the tors, they think they are safe, but they can still hear the howling of the beast.

Dimitri Coxon (13)
Hillside Special School, Plymouth

The Dark Figure In The Graveyard

The graveyard was misty. It was snowing and the ground was soggy. It was cold and windy. The thunder was rumbling. There was lightning flashing. There was a full moon. There was a flashing light in the darkness and strange noises. There was crying. There were shadows of trees in the graveyard. The trees were rattling and their scary eyes screamed.

Standing in the graveyard was a large dark figure. He was dressed in a long black coat, long-legged boots, a big black hat and black gloves. The man seemed to like the lightning rustling through the trees.

Suddenly he hurled himself at some poor lady walking through the graveyard ripping her head off. The scary eyes of the trees stared and the creatures came out. The creatures stabbed anyone at night and they stabbed the large dark figure. The murder was solved and the creatures disappeared. But they might come back.

Laura Colmer (14)
Hillside Special School, Plymouth

Is This The End?

My name is Maleeka and I live in Bangladesh. My life was always hard but today has proved the worst so far in all my twelve years of being alive. A disaster so great has caused me to see no point in life.

The disaster I speak of is flooding. Seeing my home destroyed was bad enough. It wasn't much but it was still my home. But destroyed it was. Sadly that is not the worst of it.

I'm sitting alone on a patch of earth that used to be a hill. But now as the water swirls ever closer I feel myself loosening my grip on life. Death would be a welcome fate now.

There's nothing left for me to live for. My family are all dead, my mother, father and my dear little younger brother Toby were all swept away with no hope of survival.

How fragile we are, always teetering between life and death, one slip up and we're gone forever, never to return.

I shall greet my death with open arms, for I am sure it will come soon. Anything to escape my current situation suits me. Sitting here hunched up in a ball on my little patch of earth I know this is the end.

Everything's fading, the world's turning black. But what's that noise? Is it helicopters at last come to rescue me? Or death? I'm being lifted up and up. Is this for real or just pure madness? Is this the end?

Phoebe Gwillim-Jones (12)
St Ives School, St Ives

Things Aren't What They Seem ...

The girl unpacked the last of the boxes in her new house. She reached over to switch off the radio. 'A dangerous criminal has escaped from the Hanstown Asylum,' the newsreader read out. Frantically she ran to bolt the door.

It's OK, she thought, *I have my dog to protect me.* The girl was so shaken she went straight to her bed.

A dripping noise in the bathroom kept her awake. She reached down next to her bed to check if her faithful dog was by her side. He replied by licking her hand.

In the morning the girl went to check what the dripping noise was. Her dog hung dead from the shower nozzle. Blood dripped from his neck. On the mirror written in blood were the words: *people can lick too.*

Sophie Vallance (12)
St Ives School, St Ives

The Castle And The Storm

Once upon a time there was a flying castle. One day it landed on the Cornish coast. That night there was a terrible storm, many of the fishing boats were caught out at sea. In the castle lived a lovely young ant who could see everything from the top of the castle. She ran down the stairs and called for her seahorse. She rode out above the waves and swooping down gathered the fishermen on the horse's back and took them back to the castle.

The next morning it was bright and sunny, the storm had gone. The fishermen returned to their families. The castle and the ant flew away but the fishermen would never forget the ant who was called Eia and named the town after her. Today it is called St Ives.

Steven Smith (12)
St Ives School, St Ives

The Rabbit And The Fox!

One day a young rabbit was lolloping around when he saw a fox with its head stuck in a hole in a tree. At first he froze, but then he realised that he was harmless, but he was upset and couldn't get free. So the rabbit helped him and bolted off.

Later that day the fox was out hunting with his friends, when he came to the rabbit's warren, he gasped. He didn't want him to be hurt, but he was too embarrassed to tell his friends that a mere rabbit had helped him, so he kept diverting his friends, sending them to many different places. Round and round they went, always avoiding the warren. But the other foxes were beginning to catch on.

They went home for a snack and went back, but this time the other foxes went straight to the rabbit's warren. The fox decided that his friend was more important than his pride, so he owned up and told his friends that he had been helped by a rabbit. They completely understood and left the warren alone.

And even today, so many years later, foxes will guard that warren, to protect the rabbits from the other predators that pass by.

Timmy Halliday (11)
St Ives School, St Ives

Inkleonk And Paws

It was a lovely day at the Hubbabullo Forest and little Inkleonk was sat under a mushroom eating wild berries when he saw two big green eyes staring at him through a scary bush. His little mousie whiskers pointed to the sky and he said, 'Hi Paws, what are you doing out of the kingdom of whiskers?'

'I've come here to warn you about the evil witch, that loves eating little mice like you, she's here in the forest,' the baby jaguar said happily.

Then little Inkleonk ran into something big and black with a pointy hat. *'It's the witch,'* he gasped, he hid around Paws and the witch turned into Baby Graiff.

'We tricked you!' both of them shouted and little Inkleonk went crying home.

That night he told his mother and she said, 'Don't worry, something bad will happen in return.'

The next morning Inkleonk was sat at the breakfast table when he saw the front page of the goosewaper and it had a missing sign for Paws and Baby Graiff.

Hatty Phillips (12)
St Ives School, St Ives

Remember Hedge Cutters Don't Come Out At Night

The woman checked into the hotel room with her husband. They were on their honeymoon in Jersey. They went upstairs to unpack. They kept hearing thudding noises on the ceiling; they chose to ignore it.

During the night the thudding noise got louder. They turned on the TV and watched the news. An urgent bulletin came on, 'There is a killer on the loose and he may be staying in a hotel room in Jersey'. The man looked at his wife. They turned off the TV and went to sleep.

During the night the woman heard a chainsaw, she thought it was a hedge cutter. In the morning she woke up and found her husband's head on a spike looking at her, his eyes were shocked. She got up and there was the killer on the end of the bed with a chainsaw. Then he said, *'Now it's your turn!'*

Katie Williams (11)
St Ives School, St Ives

The Wizard And The Castle

This story about a wizard called Steve, he has a staff and a sword in his hand. He travelled along the path to the scary castle. The wizard was almost there at the castle. Suddenly, he saw a bad man on the way. He took out his sword and stabbed the bad man in the heart. He was furious about what he had done so he sat down on the bench and waited for the grass to grow.

He was there at the scary castle. He walked in and saw a staircase going up to a big room with spiders' webs and a skeleton in it.

The wizard shook his head thinking he was going mad. The castle was dark, he heard a noise upstairs, suddenly the skeleton moved out of the big room down the staircase near the wizard. The wizard kicked the skeleton in the face and destroyed the body. Meanwhile he didn't go up the staircase, he went out of the scary castle and saw a very, very bad man. The wizard took his spell off the staff and the sword, and the bad man went up to the wizard, the wizard had an idea. He saw his horse under the bridge and the wizard jumped under the bridge near the horse. The horse went up to the wizard and the wizard jumped on to the horse's back and rode off on to the path heading up to his house.

Peter Trevorrow (Autistic) (11)
St Ives School, St Ives

Bluebell And The Healing River

Once in Sri Lanka there was a beautiful goddess called Bluebell. She lived amongst palm trees and her house was a handmade palm tree leaf shelter. Next to her house was a beautiful crystal flowing river which sparkled when the sun shone and it was lined with rose petals which healed.

One week in May, a giant heatwave swept over Sri Lanka taking lives in its path. Bluebell's river dried up and the animals became thirsty. Bluebell tried to nourish them by squeezing berries for them, but it was water they wanted.

One day a lady called Lola visited Bluebell on the hottest day of them all, she desperately needed healing as a doctor had told her life was running out as a mosquito had bitten her and given her the deadly disease, malaria.

Bluebell really wanted to help her but her healing river had dried up long ago. She searched through all her books and finally found a rain dance remedy. They both began running, singing and dancing until a monkey shouted, 'Hey, what are you doing?' They told him and he joined on the end. Next Tilly the tiger and Prickly the hedgehog joined on all questioning, 'What are you doing?' Suddenly a raindrop landed on Bluebell's nose and then a million more. They all rushed back to the river celebrating. When they arrived back the river was full and Lola bathed in it, finally cured they all enjoyed a glass of berry juice.

Pippa Monies (12)
St Ives School, St Ives

The Dog, The Cat And The Kennel

A dog walking along a path in Luxury Land, suddenly saw a cat in a five star kennel complete with plasma TV and a recliner chair. The dog said hi to the cat in the recliner, but the cat paid no attention to the dog and simply shut the kennel's door remotely. The dog was disgusted with the cat and trotted off to his own kennel which was only three star and had a normal chair and a normal TV. Suddenly the dog had a brilliant idea and then he went to sleep.

In the morning a high-pitched scream woke the dog up and he went to have a look. It was a turtle that had screamed. He was looking into the rude cat's kennel where the cat itself was stuck in the mechanism of the recliner, *dead.* The dog sniggered and thought back to last night's killing.

Matt Hobson (12)
St Ives School, St Ives

The Legend Of Jimmy The Reaper

Brawley looked around, thick snow covered the Moscow airport. He got into the taxi and told the taxi driver where he wanted to go. The taxi driver hesitated before driving off. Brawley was a trader from California, on a mission to collect some money off a merchant in Moscow. So Brawley made his way to the Rose Inn where he was staying the night.

When Brawley checked in he made his way up the stairs and was startled by horrifying pictures of men with no heads, dogs with bloodstained teeth and scenes of horrible execution, too terrible to even speak of. He opened the door of his bedroom and the first thing he noticed was the date, Friday 13th.

Suddenly he started to panic; he had paraskevidekatriaphobia, which meant he was scared of Friday 13th.

'Oh Brawley, Brawley, I have come for you Brawley, I'm Jimmy the Reaper.' A one-armed man wearing a mask stepped out of the wall. He had long hair and on the arm he did have, a bloodstained chainsaw was disgustingly attached.

Brawley walked slowly backwards, towards the open window.

Jimmy put his head forward and out from his fearsome mask said, 'This is the part where you run.'

Brawley stepped back, full of fear, he jumped out the open window. He fell ten storeys and died.

Many said it was a suicide but written on the walls of that very room, *'Jimmy lives again'*.

Samuel Jackson (12)
St Ives School, St Ives

Freddie Vs Jack

Freddie and Jack had always been the best of friends. They were out drinking one night, when Freddie said that his spleen was not feeling particularly well. Nothing was said about his illness for the rest of the night. Jack was having a magnificent time, getting extremely drunk. Freddie left the room briefly. Then he came back. Jack turned around and saw a masked stranger, grasping a baseball bat. *Swoosh, swoosh, bang, swoosh* ... Then Jack was knocked out.

He found himself, about 6-7 hours later, in a bath of painfully cold ice. At first, he thought he was dreaming. But no, this was for real. He looked beside him and there was a note. *'Call 999, or you will die',* is what it read. By the note was a mobile phone. He called 999 and the ambulance came immediately. *Freddie had stolen Jack's spleen!* Jack had just managed to survive. Jack never, ever, ever, ever, ever spoke to Freddie again.

And that's the way the cookie crumbles!

Billy Curtis (12)
St Ives School, St Ives

The Tree Frog And The Sugar Lump

Once upon a time there was a tree frog and this tree frog liked to eat berries; the wildest, sweetest, most colourful, juiciest berries. The tree frog's name was Marshmallow, she loved these berries so much but what she craved for every day was a sugar lump, she had only ever had a sugar lump when she was little when her mum had hopped all the way to a far away city to get one from a café. She knew a parrot that flew over the oceans and landed on cruise boats to eat some food. So one day Marshmallow asked the parrot if he could get her one. The parrot refused and flew off.

Many years later (when parrot had forgotten about Marshmallow asking for a sugar lump), Parrot was sitting up on a tree watching Marshmallow jumping on her bed of leaves with berries smeared all over her mouth.

Parrot asked for a berry out of Marshmallow's food store and Marshmallow was about to give him a berry when she remembered the time when she had asked for a sugar lump and Parrot had refused. So she said, 'OK, but just remember when I asked for a little sugar lump you wouldn't give me one.'

Marshmallow came home that night after visiting her parents' house. She found a plateful of sugar lumps.

The moral of this story is *one good turn deserves another.*

Rebecca Knee (12)
St Ives School, St Ives

Mazalamp Vs Einstein

Mazalamp was in a bar one night with his mate when he said that he wasn't feeling very well. his friend didn't take any notice. Mazalamp went home.

In the night Mazalamp woke up and went to get a glass of water when he saw a masked man, it was the evil scientist Einstein. Suddenly Einstein pulled out a chainsaw and cut off Mazalamp's ear … Mazalamp had been knocked out. Mazalamp woke up chained to a wall, he saw written on the tiles, *Call 911 or you will die!* Mazalamp found a cell phone on the floor, he picked up the phone and dialled 911, the ambulance soon came and Mazalamp was given an artificial ear. Mazalamp wanted to hunt down Einstein, he soon found him. Mazalamp went to Einstein's house, he crept up behind Einstein and slit his throat. There were no more sick mind games from Einstein. It was over!

Chris Pugh (12)
St Ives School, St Ives

The Lucky Charm

Once in the deepest part of the sea there was a man called Jim who sailed the seas with a lucky charm around his neck that he'd got from home.

One day when he was in the deep blue sea sailing along he felt the boat rocking and rocking harder and harder. All of a sudden there was a big crash from the sea, smashing against the boat and a big wave hit the boat. Jim fell out of the boat and no one has seen him since. They have found the boat and people say that if you go down into the deepest part of the sea you'll see old Jim sitting there, in a hole, where he lives quietly.

His family are happy, apart from his daughter who keeps asking for him and her mum keeps saying that he's gone on holiday. When he left to sail the seas she was two years old. She is very, very upset because she has recently found out that her dad has been dead for six years. She is angry with her mum for not telling her and she will be upset for the rest of her life. The lucky charm was not lucky at all.

Toni Chaplin (12)
St Ives School, St Ives

The Grim

There were two boys called Ricky and Jake when they had to go to New York to pick up some gold worth $1,000,000,000. So they got their stuff together and headed off to Florida airport as it took two hours to get there. They started looking for a hotel. When there were no rooms they decided to camp in the woods. They did not know about the psycho killer, the Grim Reaper.

It was approaching dawn, as they set up a fire they started hearing noises. Ricky went to go and see what it was when Jake heard, *'Argh!'*

Ricky saw a body hanging on a tree, he ran back to the fire when the Grim Reaper said, 'I m coming to kill you,' and Ricky saw he had a chainsaw, sticky black hair and blood on his chainsaw from when he sliced off Jake's head.

Ricky was petrified and shouted, *'Nooo!'* Ricky started running. It was dark and he tripped over his laces. then the Grim Reaper was there and stabbed his chainsaw right through Ricky's chest. When the police and ambulance arrived they found two bodies. It was on the news and their mums were in tears.

Charlie Rudge (12)
St Ives School, St Ives

Jack The Ripper

Just about 30 years ago, there was this boy, Jack. Everybody called him 'Jack the Ripper'. This all began when he was little. The poor child was beaten. His father hurt him every time he got a high mark in maths because his father couldn't face his child getting a high mark. Every day and every night he was hurt in some way or another, but one day (he was 18) he hit his dad back and killed him in one stroke. After the funeral Jack became really vicious. Every night he would go out and kill innocent victims and strike them and strike them with an axe until they were dead. One night he was on the bus and he saw this really pretty girl, she had longish hair with blue eyes. He went up to her and asked, 'Where are you getting off?'

'Oh, not for ages.'

'Can I sit with you?'

'Course.'

'Are you doing anything tonight?'

'Um, no, not that I know of.'

'Do you want something to eat?'

'Yeah, why not,' she said shyly.

So they got off at the next stop and went to Pizza Hut. He walked her home after.

'Thanks for tonight, it was great!'

'It's OK!'

She went back in and Jack ran home. He got out his axe and went back to her house. All that could be heard was a blood-curdling scream and the *slashing* of an axe.

Becky Nankervis (12)
St Ives School, St Ives

A Day In The Life Of Michael Schumacher

It seemed a normal day for me, just another opportunity to stand on top of the podium. Little did I know I would be laying in a hospital bed fighting for my life! I got up and had my breakfast, cereal and toast. I got dressed and said goodbye to my wife and kids. She didn't like me racing, she never told me that but I could tell by the look in her eyes every time I went to race. She would be along later but I just didn't like leaving her or the kids.

Which car to choose, that was a big part of going to work. I'd narrowed it down to two, the Ferrari 360 Spyder or the Lamborghini Diablo. The doors made me choose the Lambo; I just had to go to work in style. We were trying to outdo each other before we even got to the track.

I got in, got all my leathers on and was raring to go. I was fifth on the grid, not bad, but it's not where you start that matters it's where you finish that's really important.

The warm up lap was perfect; the car was working just how I liked it. The car just seemed to glide. Barichello was in 7th, two places behind me, if we worked well together we could become first and second, hopefully me first!

Red ... green, go, go, go, into second, then third. 100mph braking into the first corner. Button hit me. *Argh!. Boom ...*

Reece Mills (13)
St James' High School, Exeter

A Day In The Life Of Samuel Lemon

Sam is seven years old, he is very small for his age. He has blue eyes and is blond. Sam also has a problem. He has spina bifida. He goes to Whipton School, he is in Year 2 at the moment, almost in Year 3. Sam has two dogs, two cats and two hamsters that he shares with his two sisters, Jodie, aged 13 and Stephanie, aged 9.

Sam's favourite foods are fish cake and chips and flapjack and custard. Sam's able to play like other kids but he just can't run, he tries his best though. Most of Sam's strength is in his arms, he uses his arms the most as he is in a wheelchair sometimes. He loves to play outside in the front of the house with all the other kids, he loves to play rugby, football, golf and riding on his scooter, but he needs a bit of help with that. Sam's able to walk at the moment with splints to support his legs but we do not know if he will be able to walk when he's older.

Jodie Lemon (13)
St James' High School, Exeter

Shock Shot

Commander John Walker woke to the sound of gunfire and explosions. He got dressed slowly as he dreaded the day ahead.

Another day of possible death, kidnapping or torture. He reluctanctly grabbed his rifle and slipped out of his tent. He was greeted at the trench as he sat down to watch the base.

Sergeant Smithers grabbed him and explained the day's work to him, he and his team were to finish the war ... infiltrate the base, kidnap their leader and hold him until Iran surrendered.

John assembled his elite team for battle. He looked at his star troops, knowing he would not see half of them ever again!

The jeep slowly rolled along the desert sands to the tents laid out in rows of ten, the flight had been exhausting but when the time came John was more awake than he had been for a long while.

The troops surrounded the tent, guns at the ready. It was well past one in the morning so the leader should have been asleep.

They slipped in and grabbed him, John covered his mouth, Private Mittens grabbed his arms and Smith grabbed his legs, the other team members flanked them. He managed to push John's hand off and started to shout!

The team ran for the jeep as the Iranian soldiers shot at John ...

'Argh!' A hit, John fell to the ground bleeding and thinking of the family he had left behind.

Timothy Hannah (13)
St James' High School, Exeter

A Day In The Life Of George W Bush

Woke up. Thought, *that wasn't too bad, I should do that more often.* Got out of bed. Ate a pretzel, choked. Survived thanks to my nanny. Thought again, *ouch, that one hurt.* Phone rang. Fell downstairs, hurt less than thinking. Picked up phone; it was Tony. Talked for ten seconds, realised I was hungry, put down phone. Ran into fridge, that was cold, tasted like pretzels. Finished eating.

Security came to escort me to board meeting. Walked into room, tripped over. Sat down, chatted to vice president. Insulted Tony Blair, looked at camera, realised it was on. Looked blankly at camera for ten minutes, turned away. Got bored, pressed big red button for fun. Nearly started WWIII.

Tony Blair called again, he sounded funny so I laughed, put down the phone again. Discussed the war in Iraq. Got bored so I laughed again.

Walked out of meeting because I was hungry, met with wife. Forgot her name. Gave her my vacant look for twenty minutes. Must get flowers. Why am I getting flowers again? Wife shouted at me. Must get expensive flowers.

Had conference with protesters, they shouted at me. Remembered wife's name. Protesters continued to shout at me. Finished conference. Wiped off rotten food from suit. Changed suit. Forgot wife's name again. Got attacked by protesters, had to change suit again. Walked into fridge again. Went for a bike ride. Fell off. I really should learn, maybe some other time. Apologised to security guard; I don't know why but I was bored; it was something to do. Got bored again, started a war.

Misha Vertkin (13)
St James' High School, Exeter

A Day In The Life Of The Queen

One gets up early and gets one's servants to get one's clothes ready. One must look good always. One is never late, everyone else is simply early. One drinks tea with one's little finger poking out and eats biscuits. One gets one's hair cut. After one's hair is looking dazzling, one will sit on the throne looking important, while being painted.

At 11am that *ghastly* Tony Blair gave one some papers to sign. *Boring!* Only another 150 papers left to sign. One had better ring one's bell, One wants tea. One has 75 papers left to sign. When's lunchtime? Ring bell again, one wants more tea. 50 papers left and 20 minutes left 'til lunch. *Servant,* one wants more tea. 25 papers left, 10 minutes 'til lunch. Finished.

Servant, one understands it's lunchtime now. One has been seated for lunch and is relaxing while one's servants get food prepared. Yum, food. After lunch one must go with Prince Charles to knight Paul McCartney and Ellen MacArthur. One is now full up, one wants more tea. Servant, fetch one's tea. Time to knight Paul McCartney.

Chloe Meredith (13)
St James' High School, Exeter

Adventure At Sea

One summer's day in Hawaii, three girls were sailing over to find some treasure. Lucie, who was the oldest, suddenly called out to Abi and Ellie. 'Hey, look there's the treasure island. Let's hurry.'

So the girls quickly paddled over to the island. When they'd got there the youngest child, Ellie, shouted out, 'There's the treasure, let's get it.' So with Lucie in front they ran over. Suddenly a pirate jumped out in front of them.

'Aye, I am Captain Termite-Leg, thank you for finding my treasure.'

'Your treasure?' cried Abi. 'We found it, not you.'

'Tough, go away and leave my treasure alone.'

The girls backed away but didn't go over to the boat. They hid in the forest, where Lucie had an idea.

'Why don't we go back and start a fire to burn that pirate's wooden leg?' So that's what the girls did. When they got back to where the captain was, they quickly set up the fire and called the captain over.

'Oi, Termite-Leg, come over here a minute,' Abi cried, 'we've got a present for you.'

'What do you want?' the captain yelled. At that moment Ellie got a burning log from the fire and set Captain Termite-Leg's wooden leg alight.

The captain didn't have time to run. He quickly burned to the ground. The girls celebrated, then quickly loaded the treasure and sailed home.

Jade Ashelford (13)
St James' High School, Exeter

Death Road

They left home, Billy, Bilbo and Fado were going to their mate's house to have a wild night out. They had heard about 'Death Road' but they didn't believe anything about it. But what they didn't know was that whoever goes up 'Death Road' never comes back ...

They stopped on the way at a local supermarket. They bought some alcohol for their wild night out. They got back into their car and drove up the winding roads.

'Hey, Bilbo what do you think about Death Road?' sniggered Billy.

'I'm really scared, I think we should take the other road,' joked Bilbo.

Death Road was coming up, getting closer ...

'Guys, I think something is wrong with the car,' said Fado. Suddenly there was a bang and the car stopped. They looked at each other.

'Urgh! Why can't you get a better car?' shouted Billy.

'Shut up! You didn't have to come!' said Fado. Billy got out the car and walked off up Death Road.

'Stuff him, we can go without him.' They waited 20 minutes for someone to come but no one came, it was deserted.

Suddenly there was a scream. It was coming from the road.

'Let's go have a look,' said Bilbo. They walked up and heard another, 'Argh!' Then it got quieter. They ran into the woods and kept running ... they stopped and there hanging from a branch was Billy ...

Two weeks later, three men were missing, named Frado, Bilbo and Billy.

Joshua Grimes (13)
St James' High School, Exeter

A Day In The Life Of Tony Blair

I had to dive out of bed early, it was a really busy, important day that lay ahead. I was meeting with the seven most powerful men in the world. We met for a hearty breakfast and a photo shoot. Right, now down to business, we had lots to discuss.

Everything was going well when my secretary came in to tell me my day was going to be unforgettable but for all the wrong reasons. Terrorists had set off bombs in London, the first one must have gone off whilst I was enjoying my breakfast. *Oh no, what do I do now?*

The helicopter landed, my stomach churned. What was I going to say, or more importantly, what was I going to see? The news has just sunk in. Seven people have already died. I could so do without it today of all days.

Chirac, Putin, Bush were amazing. I couldn't believe the support they gave me. As soon as we landed we went to Downing Street. By now every TV channel was showing the news.

Terri Cainey (13)
St James' High School, Exeter

Fight For Victory (FFV)

I had been in the army now for seven years, but today was a day like no other, the words which everyone had feared were announced, 'The world is at war'. The world went silent, so silent that you could have heard a pin drop.

It felt like my stomach was going to come out of my mouth. My commander called my troops and me. He told us to go to our tents and pack our bags, he said we had an hour to pack them and be on our way to Germany. I packed my rations, spare clothes and my guns and first-aid kit.

We then flew over to Germany and landed in an airfield. We set up our tents and sleeping bags, and waited for nightfall.

It felt like we waited for hours, it was slowly getting darker and darker.

It was time, the time we had all been waiting for, we loaded our planes and shot off into the air. Our aim was to knock Berlin flat, so that all that was left was rubble and dust. We had two miles to our target, the very centre of Berlin.

We were there right above our target and we let them go. We watched them fall then, *bang, bang!* We had hit our target, we then had the task of getting back to our hideout. We had left Berlin but then did something none of us had expected. Their planes came up behind us and were shooting at our rear. We shot back and then they just exploded. We were safe but we still had the challenge of landing. We turned around as we were well past our expected landing point, we could feel the plane getting lower and lower.

We landed safely and for the rest of the war it was just like that, instead though I kept thinking about my friends and family.

The day I had waited for had come at last. The war was over and I could go home to my family and see my friends.

James Parmenter (13)
St James' High School, Exeter

Untitled

Timmothy was a clever boy. He'd just finished some rather hard exams at school and was having a week off on holiday in Malta with his parents to celebrate his success; he had an extremely rich family. Timm went to a grammar school, paid for by his parents.

On holiday, Timm was taking an evening stroll, while his parents were at the hotel writing postcards to their friends. While strolling, Timmothy noticed a shiny green corner of something sticking out of the mud. He dug away some of the soil, revealing more of the bizarre article. It appeared to be a triangular prism of about two inches long. The triangular face was roughly three inches along one edge. Timm inserted the object into his rucksack and continued his stroll.

A short while later, he heard a loud, annoying buzzing sound coming from his rucksack. He took it off his back and opened it. A small, green monkey emerged from beneath his 'Robert The Rabbit' comic.

'Hee, hee, hee, hee,' giggled the monkey, 'you have done well in your exams delicious young boy, which is why I must now eat you, so that your knowledge can be transferred into my brain to enable me to take over the world! Hee, hee, hee, hee.'

'No!' exclaimed Timm. 'You cannot! ... Argh!'

'Hee, hee, hee, hee, yum, yum, this child is tasty.' Then the monkey went on to conquer New Zealand. When his conquering days were over, he had the raising of his children to take care of.

Simon Johns (14)
St Luke's High School, Exeter

A Day In The Life Of Steve Spindleshanks

Hello! I'm Steve Spindleshanks and I'm a cat. Actually I'm a rather splendid tabby cat, but modesty prevents me from giving you a clearer picture! I'm sure you would be very impressed if you met me!

I live in St Thomas. I had hoped for something a bit grander, but times have been hard, and Mummy has been doing her best.

Normally I rise in the morning at roughly 7am. This allows me to remind Mummy to serve up my delicious Eukanuba ASAP! Usually she is very well behaved, but recently she has been lying in. A little nibble often hurries her up.

When Mummy and Lucy have left for work, the house is very quiet, so in order to keep boredom at bay, I seize the opportunity to write poetry.

I bet you are thinking, *can this cat have any more talents?* The answer is *yes!* I will have you know that I am an extremely musical cat and, every day without fail, I have a tinkle on the old ivories! Lucy also plays the piano; I like to think of myself as her inspiration.

Some afternoons I find myself nibbling on a catnip teabag or sleeping. (Usually both, as one tends to lead to another!)

At teatime I normally find Lucy or Mummy sitting down, so once I have tucked in heartily to my Eukanubes, I snuggle up on a lap, as I know they need some love and attention after a long day's work.

After tea, I patrol the neighbourhood, checking everything is in order. I never get into fights, as I would not want to hurt or humiliate anyone! Lucy sees this act of kindness as retreat. How wrong can she be?

Lucy Foote (14)
St Luke's High School, Exeter

Untitled

Mr Finlind stepped out of his BMW, stretched and walked to the farm gate where he was greeted by a tall, 60-year-old woman.
'Greetings, Ms Inkrah I presume?' Finlind asked.
'Welcome to my farms!' Inkrah shouted.
Looking confused, Finlind pulled out a notepad and asked,
'So, tell me about these farms of yours.'
Inkrah stood straight with both arms at her sides and shouted,
'All 10,000 children are working on four farms, all the farms are guarded by six canons!'
Looking slightly concerned about Inkrah's last statement, Finlind asked, 'These canons of yours, they are for protection I assume?'
With no hesitation Inkrah sharply replied, 'No!' Finland jumped at the volume of Inkrah's voice.
'Child try to escape! Canon fire! Thus killing child.' Finlind suddenly became very aware of how unsafe he was.
'This canon firing has never happened before has it?' Inkrah's face suddenly became stronger and a smile grew slowly across her face.
'Only once, child ran very fast, north he went, my partner Akrahz noticed him run so ... *bang, bang* went canons, *bang, bang, bang* they went, killing many, many children. It was a very happy day for all.'
Finland became very frightened by this story and ran for his BMW, dropping his notepad in the process.
'You'll return!' Inkrah shouted. As the BMW drove full speed away from the gates, Inkrah muttered, 'you forgot your trousers.'
Inkrah picked up the trousers, turned around to the farm and walked through the gates.
'These will be good for children's food tonight.'
And the cast iron gates of Hell closed behind her.

Josh Clarkin (15)
St Luke's High School, Exeter

A Day In The Life Of A Cat

In the morning I wake up, go out and catch myself some breakfast, like a mouse or a fish from next-door's garden pond. Then I go for a little walk round the house, looking for a nice quiet spot to have a nice nap and dream of something nice.

After about an hour or so I wake up and it's dinner time. My owner gets me a small tin of lamb and chicken, which I really enjoy and never leave a spot of. Then it's off to the park to watch the kids play football and relax in the warm fresh air.

Around 5pm I go home to play with my owners. I really love a wind-up mouse, they look so real and I wish they were! By now I'm starting to get a bit hungry, so out I go to catch me another mouse or maybe a bird if I'm lucky. Off I go.

It's started getting darker earlier now, so I have to get home earlier, which I don't like because it's boring just stuck inside with no mates to talk to or play with. And that is my day. You may think it's boring but it's not for a cat like me, *miaow!*

Luke Plain (14)
St Luke's High School, Exeter

The Face

I was walking through the cloud of dust with my squad, wondering whether I would live or whether I would have to kill. I didn't want to die! I have three children at home and my wife is pregnant again. I don't want to kill because I couldn't live with myself.

My army general warned me to be careful but then I heard him cry out. I followed the sound and I saw his face. I checked for a pulse but found none. Standing up I looked around me. *Bang!* I felt the earth move.

That was the first explosion and it was so close that I could taste the gas. Turning I ran for my life; my sergeant saw me and shouted, 'Get back in there!' But I took no notice and carried on running.

Suddenly, I came to a forest; *should I go through the forest and be in danger of being ambushed or should I go around to see if there is another way out?* I decided to go around, so I started off at a jog but then I smelt the smell of the burnt iron given off by a gun. I dropped to the ground and moments later a body fell on top of me. Seconds later, I noticed that it was my best friend. I started to cry; I moved his body off of mine, ran into the forest and climbed a tree. I cried out, 'Why did it have to be him?' ...

Kylie Hardwick (14)
St Luke's High School, Exeter

Flying Pigs

There once was an old lady, who swore she'd seen a flying pig. Everybody laughed in her face and told her she was mad. They even tried putting her into a mental home, but they wouldn't accept her. They said that they only took people with serious issues, not a joke that an old lady was playing.

So she went home to her house in the middle of the moors, near Okehampton. At first it was only at random times that she would see this pig flying above her house, then it turned into every week, then every day.

So she called her friend on Sunday and told her to come over. They sat and waited for the pig to fly over as usual. It did, the old lady's friend believed her and they showed the people that lived close to her and the pigs became her pets.

Deborah Kellaway (14)
St Luke's High School, Exeter

A Day In The Life Of A Hobo

I woke up this morning and I was soaking wet. I think I got peed on, those flipping drunks. What did I do?

It's not easy you know. The other night the 'pigs' moved me three times and it was chucking it down. Now I'm stood on the street corner begging. I could be here for two hours before I get £2.

All I want is a cheese roll and a biscuit. It's like this all the time, begging from 9.30am to 9pm, with a few breaks to get some food, if I have been given enough money.

Jordan Westcott (13)
St Luke's High School, Exeter

The Scrap Book
(An extract)

Buzz. The rusty school bell announced that it was break time. Daisy hated that sound. She put her favourite pink schoolbag on her aching back and dragged herself to the toilets.

Every break and lunchtime Daisy would try and spend as much time as possible in the toilets. She would sit on the toilet with her scrapbook. This was her most treasured possession. Her mum started it when Daisy was a baby, putting her newborn pictures in it and her hospital identity band. As she grew older Daisy carried it on. Especially when her mum died, she started putting everything in it. Soon it told her life story, even though there was not much to tell.

The door opened and the sound of the pretty, popular girls filled the bathroom. They came in on schedule three times a day. They hogged the mirrors, brushing their glossy hair and applying coat after coat of lipgloss.

Daisy hated hearing their stories about which boy pulled which girl, that sort of thing. She decided to put her scrapbook into her overloaded bag and leave.

'Who's that?' asked Chrissie, the richest girl in school.

'Only this geek in my year,' replied Lucy, 'she's not worth knowing.'

Daisy, wiping a tear from her eye, went to wait outside the science lab.

Later that evening, she was looking at her scrapbook on her bed while the words, *she's not worth knowing*, echoed in her head.

Ruby Fuller (11)
Torpoint Community School, Torpoint

The Goblet Of Mortuguay
(An extract)

One upon a time, in a land far, far away, there was a glorious kingdom called Mortuguay. There were tall houses and wonderful gardens. If you walked past one all you would smell for days would be the scent of roses on a summer's day. If you visited the kingdom you would think it was peaceful and harmonious; but it was far from that. The kingdom was threatened by the Virigons - terrifying, fire-breathing dragons. The Virigons had tried in vain to invade this wonderful country and make all the villagers and even King Garapool, their slaves. Some people had been taken and the older villagers talked about a beautiful princess who had disappeared many years ago.

This disaster would have occurred if their ancestors hadn't found a way of stopping them. They asked the elves to make a magic goblet, which would stop anything that could be the root of a tragic end to the kingdom. The Goblet of Mortuguay was made of solid gold and shimmered under the summer's sun like ripples on a deep, peaceful pond. It was studded with rubies as red as the setting sun and emeralds, as green as crisp leaves swaying in the wind.

Thomas Harry (12)
Torpoint Community School, Torpoint

Connie's Adventures

The sun started to rise, I was feeling hungry. None of my owners were awake. I strolled to the cat flap. A bird was perched on a branch of a tree. I pounced; it flew away. I managed to chase it round the garden but I couldn't catch it.

Suddenly I heard a deep rumbling noise. It was coming from next door. Slowly I turned around. A huge grey dog was staring at me, its mouth was vibrating, drool dripped. What could I do?

Run.

I ran. I ran past many birds but yet I couldn't stop to eat them or else it might have been the last meal I ever ate. Then I would be the dog's meal.

It felt like I had been running for days. My legs felt like sticks. My lungs felt like they had shrivelled up. I jumped into a bush. I stayed there for ages until I discovered it was fine to come out.

I looked around. Where was I? Suddenly I had a great idea; if I climbed a tree I would be able to see our greenhouse.

I managed to climb the tree but the house was nowhere in sight. I was just about to get down when the ground went blurry. I was stuck!

Amy Fishwick (12)
Torpoint Community School, Torpoint

Description Of Holes
(Inspired by the film 'Holes')

It is absolute hell here. I have blisters from head to toe. My hands are sore and blistered. This is all because of my no-good, dirty-rotten, pig-stealing, great, great grandfather. The other boys in my department are horrible. Zero's quite nice but the others are horrible.

The scorching heat is as intense as the fires of Hell itself! The land around is completely barren and there are no plants or animals for miles around, apart from the odd one or two yellow-spotted lizards. I thought Mr Pendanski would have given me the day off when I found the fossil. I don't know why we should dig hundreds of holes. Maybe it is because the warden is looking for something. I feel like breaking down and crying.

Ben Ayres (12)
Torpoint Community School, Torpoint

Deadly Double Won By Villa

Elburton Villa 3-0 Saltash United Under 12 Vanguard Cup Final.

Elburton Villa were going into the final having already won the league. They were up against a side who have gone through twists and turns throughout the season, but were the only team to beat Villa in the league. The odds were all on Elburton's side and it paid off with a comfortable 3-0 win. Ben Hudson started the match off with a well-worked goal just five minutes from the start. The second goal got Elburton's hopes up even more when Swain slotted in a neat finish from inside the box. Shortly after half-time Villa were awarded a penalty for a handball, Seb Broomfield stepped up. The keeper went the right way but sadly he tapped it over his head. 3-0. It looked like they were champions but Saltash put in every inch of effort, with some sharp attacks. But Villa defended well right to the end and were able to lift the trophy right up, to their delight. We heard from Charlie Legg, Villa's manager, 'Well we deserved the win, they fought hard right to the end. I am very pleased with the lads and can't wait 'til next season'.

Lewis Allan (12)
Torpoint Community School, Torpoint

A Day In The Life Of Someone In A Tsunami

It was coming fast and furious, crashing down the streets like a bolt of lightning. I froze on the spot, I couldn't move, couldn't even breathe. Then I turned and ran. I ran like I'd never ran before. People ran beside me, clutching their loved ones and shrieking at the thought of death lying in the path ahead. I turned around. There it was, a huge wave racing faster than the wind, destroying the weak wooden houses standing at the sides of the street. It hit me with a smack and the murky brown water swept me down the street.

As I slowly closed my eyes, the last image I saw was that wave, the wave that ended my life.

Megan Marshall (11)
Torpoint Community School, Torpoint

A Day In The Life Of A Teenager In WWII

Buildings, houses destroyed, but what can I do to help? Nothing. The cries and screams of the innocent people all huddled together, praying perpetually for this disaster to stop. The sky is as black as a piece of coal. Please tell me, when is it going to end?

The ground is covered in mire and the stench of the bodies makes my stomach turn. Buildings, shops, homes, trees, all destroyed. I feel so helpless. Children are looking around for scraps off the floor. People are standing on pieces of glass which have been shattered from the windows of buildings. Though what makes me really feel tense is innocent people's bodies amongst all the rubble. It's like a graveyard. My eyes are stinging continuously and I can barely breathe because of all the dust building up gradually in the back of my throat. I just sit there hoping, praying for it to stop, whilst laying my head upon my mother's lap. I see a tear run down her face. I ask if she is OK. She says softly that she's fine. I know she is just putting on a brave face for me. I lay there trying to take my mind off things but as I do I can hear the sound of another building go down. It's like a living nightmare! All I want to know is, why?

Silence starts to build up and as I look around I can see people grouped together wearing rags, with hardly any food to eat. I sit there staring at my mum's face. She's just staring, staring at the rubble that used to be our home, but now it's all gone.

As the day comes to an end a silence is around me. People sleeping, people praying and people huddled together, keeping each other warm. I just stare. It's like a ghost town. All I can do is pray. But what I want to know most of all is, when is it going to end?

Sophie Palmer (14)
Torpoint Community School, Torpoint

PJ Pooch

She was motionless. Eyelids fixed shut with superglue.

Around the orange painted dining room there were scattered toys: balls, bones, bitten rope, soft toys, hard toys, even one beneath the pooch who laid to the side of a wooden table engraved with pen markings.

She was still motionless as Fred moved closer to the dog. He stroked her.

Suddenly, without warning, she opened her eyes and darted her head towards Fred's hand. She licked him.

Fred stubbed out his cigarette, which he held in one hand, so he could stroke PJ with both hands.

'Night girl,' he said softly as he turned his back on PJ, left the room and made his way up the stairs where a warm, cosy bed waited for him.

Fred awoke hours later. He could see his bedside clock. 2am it read. But he was not interested in the time - he was interested in the smoke entering his bedroom.

'PJ, PJ!' he bellowed but PJ could not hear him.

He sprinted down the stairs, missing a few on the way, unlocked the door, which was stubborn to open, and ran as fast as a cheetah down the garden, now illuminated by the flames. He looked back at the house.

'PJ, PJ!' he cried as he hung his head. Had the dog perished? Would he ever see his companion of nine years again?

Then from the smoke a hazy silhouette appeared. Could it be? It was. His loving companion was back.

Michael Ives (12)
Torpoint Community School, Torpoint

A Day In The Life
(An extract)

For as long as I could remember I adored flying. My father had been a highly successful pilot before he retired and, from a young age had captained me to far off destinations; filled with the smell of aromatic spices or the chill of a snowflaked wind. The sweltering summer of 2001 was nearly over. I was due to fly home, back to England from my aunt's Texas ranch dotted with auburn dust-filled fields and smoking bulls charging unceremoniously at passing tourists, bearing hands to pat their backs only to turn blood-red as the bulls' towering bodies charged at them. My job was to feed the heated animals whilst catching a few rays from the midday sun. Aunty had the pleasure of not doing this job as she had sprained her leg, when cleaning out her old barn ready for it to be converted.

Crowds of business-like men and women who filled the airport, carrying damaged briefcases and wearing an expression of such importance, barged past me. Screaming children brattily ordered their parents into submission: demanding the same lolly that passed minutes earlier in the grips of a smug-looking toddler. I saw at least twenty holidaymakers walk past proudly, sporting an over-produced brand of Texan cowboy hat. Each like the other; pink and perched precariously upon its occupant's head. That day did not see one individual, all too stereotypical to be unique. This was all true apart from that boy. The boy whose eyes melted into mine, gazing with pearly blueness; the boy whose mouth bore a perfect line of teeth; the boy who owned my final stare.

Bethanie Dwyer (14)
Torpoint Community School, Torpoint

I Am Invisible
(An extract)

I am invisible. I took my own life to save another. One good deed before I went. At least I know they haven't forgotten me. I can still see them.

Why me though! Can someone tell me? Can anyone answer these questions?

My name is Belinda Clearwater and I am 14 years old. I won't get any older. Some people might like that, but not me, not now. I just couldn't stand there and watch Claire get taken by the warm, rich flames. So I got her out. Unfortunately for me, the house collapsed before I could get out to safety. Everyone saw it happen, my mum, my dad, my sister, Claire, Lisa and Danny, my boyfriend.

Well anyway, back to my present self. I died on that night and now I am here looking down on all of my friends. It is exactly one year from that dreadful night. I have seen and heard everything that Claire and Lisa have told everyone. It all started the day after the fire.

'Claire, Claire!' said a soft voice. Lisa Damoon leant over the stiff body of her sister Claire. 'Claire wake up!'

Claire's eyes slowly opened. Her stunning blue eyes pierced through the faint white light. 'Lisa?' Claire's croaky voice replied.

'I'm here,' returned Lisa from Claire's calling.

'Where's Belinda? Is she okay?'

'Um, Claire, Belinda didn't make it. She got lost in the fire. She saved you and lost her own life. It was a very brave thing that she did. She won't be forgotten. Never.'

'Oh my God. Why did she save me? How's her family? How's Danny?'

'They're fine. Upset, but they are coping.'

'Oh this has all gone wrong. Why did Belinda go in there and save me? It should have been me!' cried Claire.

'Hey don't speak like that. It's all over now. Yes, it's sad but we have to get on with our lives. It's no good worrying about it. Now get some rest,' said Lisa, stepping quietly away from the bed.

Sarah Day (14)
Torpoint Community School, Torpoint

School

School, the best years of your life. Yeah right! All that work and as for sticking to the rules that s no easy task I can tell you. I mean we spend the majority of our childhood taking the long journey from being a child to becoming an adult at school and teachers expect you to keep to the rules and not mess about. One of my favourite sayings teachers commonly use is 'grow up'. It's like, hello, we are children, *jeez!*

Amidst all the doom and gloom you can always count on a good laugh at lunchtime. There's always at least one fight during the summer term once the 'hooligans' are unleashed onto the school field. Everyone makes such a big deal about a 'fight'. The whole field is automatically drawn towards the so-called scrap. Dinner ladies try to run to the rescue. Sadly, no matter how much they try to make it look like they are getting there in some sort of urgency, it is always over by the time they arrive at the scene.

After all the commotion and hard work we are given a variety of protein packed and nutritionally filled meals. Such as chips swimming in grease, burgers apparently made of rubber and a jacket potato thrown in to make it look healthy.

Lily Gillman (15)
Torpoint Community School, Torpoint

Murder Alley

It was a dark night. All was quiet in Park Avenue. The road behind is called Woodland Way, otherwise known as 'Murder Alley'. It was quiet there too. Maybe too quiet. The street lights shone on the cold concrete. I was looking out of my window into the starry sky.

Suddenly, a loud hammering on the door woke me from my hypnotic state. I crept downstairs feeling weary. I peered through the peephole and to my complete surprise it was a police officer. I thought to myself, *what would a police officer want with me at this hour?*

'Hello Officer, how can I help?' I mumbled.

'Hello there, we are just inquiring about the man that was murdered outside your home three weeks ago,' he said demandingly, 'it's just routine; however, we have reason to believe that you were involved.'

'Well officer I have got news for you, I have had nothing to do with the murder.'

'Well we have reason to believe that you have, so if you wouldn't mind we would appreciate it if you would come to the police station for questioning.'

'What happens if I say no?'

'I will arrest you!'

'Well I'm not coming because I didn't do it!'

'Tom Sally, I am arresting you on suspicion of murder, you do not have to say anything but it may harm your defence if you do not mention when questioned something which you later rely on in court, anything you do say may be given in evidence …'

David Flint (15)
Torpoint Community School, Torpoint

A Day In The Life Of A Victim Of Bullying!

The shrill scream of the alarm told me it was time for my daily ordeal to begin again. *I must not be beaten by them; I must not be beaten by them.*' I repeated my daily mantra in a vain attempt to convince myself, but who was I kidding?

I pulled my clothes off the hanger, dreading the day ahead of me. Butterflies started to build up inside of me. I started putting my clothes on so slowly, if I put them on any slower then I would stop.

I finally finished getting changed. I took a deep breath and walked down the stairs. Mum had my breakfast on the table ready for me but my stomach couldn't take it. Mum asked what was wrong with me. I was tempted to tell her but I just couldn't face it.

I took my first step out of the front door dreading every minute of it. I slowly dragged my feet, watching people laughing and joking with their friends. I wish that was me.

There she was. At the school gate with her cronies. Her hair was scraped up into a ponytail. She was wearing a shirt that showed her belly piercing and a skirt that only just covered her bum. Everyone fancied her and she knew it.

I walked past her with my head held high. She stopped right in front of me and says, 'Look at the state of that,' they all just started giggling.

I felt so small. I turned around and the popular gang stood there and heard everything. How embarrassing. They all laughed and walked past me making a silly remark.

I wish I had someone I could trust to talk to. I just want to move on and put the past behind me.

Leanne Stevens (15)
Torpoint Community School, Torpoint

Deserted In A New World

It was the first day of school for me. New school, new city and a new start. The ground was covered in sticky gum and rubbish. It's different from my last home. I was engulfed by people, barging past not even caring about me. It was like a field of bulls charging into each other, it was like everyone was crowded into the vacant space. Screaming little girls, skaters riding past, adults rushing to get to work.

As I approached the giant gate, time sped past; the bells rang as I stood there dazed in a new world. I looked around, all the kids had gone inside and the playground was like a desert, nothing sounded except for the silent whispers of the wind.

I slowly walked across the smouldering tarmac, it was like a black river. I entered the school; all I could see was a long corridor with a wooden door at the end. I walked briskly down the stone floor, it was so beautiful to look at. I approached the door and grabbed the handle. All I could think was, *does this door await my fate?*

Yasmin Carson (14)
Torpoint Community School, Torpoint

Short Story

Briskly walking through the busy city streets, my mum and I were on the way to the train station preparing to say our goodbyes. I'm used to the city. All of the pushing and the yelling of all the busy people in a rush to get to the places they need to be. None of this was new to me. But soon I would be on the long, horrid steam train on the way to meet my temporary family until the war was over.

As we arrived at the train station I was watching all of the distraught families, crying and promising that they will be together again. Mum suddenly touched my shoulder and said, 'Well, here we are.' She tried to put a brave smile on her face but it wasn't too convincing as a thick tear began to slowly trickle down her cheek. Mum slowly knelt down to the floor and tied her long arms around me as if she would never let go. I didn't want her to but I understood that she had to.

The loud whispers of the train in the distance were getting louder and louder and the fumes of the thick smoke began to get stronger. The train changed to a sudden screech as it came to a painful halt. Mum began to escort me to the train doors and I could feel the hairs on the back of my neck stand on end.

Finally, I stepped up into the train as I heard Mum shout, 'I'll see you soon Mary, I promise.' After hearing her say that my eyes began to build up with tears and a cold shiver ran through my spine.

I managed to find an empty seat inside an empty room; right alongside the small square window near where Mum was standing. I dumped my bags on the shelves and then sat myself down whilst taking a deep breath, trying to reassure myself.

Emily Hall (15)
Torpoint Community School, Torpoint

Time Capsule

Here we are in the year 3000. A lot has changed. *Where are we? I can't see two feet in front of my face, I can't breathe. Is this what lies ahead for our future children?*

The air is thick with pollution. It's like walking through a street after the war where the air iss thick with dust, smoke and sea fog.

In front I see a pearl-white gate. For why is it here? The smell becomes fragrant and the air as clean as an autumn morning as the dew glistens. *Where are we? Where are we?*

As we pass the gates the view becomes clear. Parents and children playing happily in their gardens. The emerald grass twinkles as the air brushes by. The blue sky is as clear as crystal, never dull or interrupted, dazed is the world as to what has become of it.

For is this a new upon the old? A new ozone put upon the broken one? The air is pure oxygen, no one smokes here, everyone is the perfect weight. Everything is perfect. A new perfect world in an imperfect universe.

The only difference is the sound. There is none. How can a perfect world be silent? We have been walking for 5/6 hours, not a sound or a shop anywhere. Except wait for it … 'New World Chip', can this be a shop?

This is the future ID. A chip in the back of the neck like a cat or dog, why? A good way to record all our people, but why now? There aren't that many people here anyway.

Beth Hunt (15)
Torpoint Community School, Torpoint

Her Life Was Hell

I walked dragging my feet behind me as my slow strides led me down the back lane; the wind blowing the leaves off the trees, it was just another day that I feared.

In the distance the gates loomed ominously, the ones I walked through every day; the ones where all my trouble started.

My life, one that I wish I never had. Why me? I asked this question every day. Why me? I was always the one no one liked, no one respected, the one everyone picked on.

Heart racing, fingers trembling as I saw her piercing eyes look right through me. My only support was the black cat which purred against my feet. It was Friday 13th, but every day seemed like Friday 13th to me. Every bit of bad luck was thrown in my direction.

The bell rang, my feet tapped and my heart raced as I approached my first lesson. Alone, sad, frightened and scared, my emotions running wild.

'Loner, loser,' all these names calling at me as I walked down the corridor. Being pushed into the lockers; getting my money stolen and all I could think of was 3.20 when the bell rang and I went home dreading what was to come on Monday.

The day dragged on and as lunchtime approached the sun beamed and there was not a cloud to be seen in the sky. As much as I wanted to go outside I couldn't, I feared what was around the corner. So ... I sat in the library reading my book as the sun scorched onto my back. I wished this wasn't the way my life was. The bell rang for last lesson which went quickly as it was a test, but then when the bell rang to go home my heart raced; my whole body shivered. I ran to the car where my mum picked me up. Year 8 and I still couldn't walk home by myself. I got home and sat down, all I could think of was Monday.

Callie Jenkins (14)
Torpoint Community School, Torpoint

A Day In The Life Of A Homeless Man

Begging was his life. A boring one at that. All John had was a little pet dog called Scraps. Frowning faces passed John as he sat in the same doorway every single day. There were muffled voices of grumpy old people, cursing at him as they looked down their snooty noses. Stuck up. That's what they were. Stuck up.

The smells of fast food lingered in the air. But, he never had enough money to satisfy his stomach. Scraps also spent his days with the continuous feeling of hunger.

Maddison Nixon (14)
Torpoint Community School, Torpoint

A Day In The Life Of A Giant Vietnamese Panda

A documentary exploring one day in the life of a giant Vietnamese panda.

6am   Giant Vietnamese panda awakes in the forests of Da Nang. The weather is mild. The temperature is moderate, the sun rises slowly. The giant Vietnamese panda rises and tumbles through the dense forestry. There are no other Giant Vietnamese pandas to be seen. They are very rare. Even in Da Nang. Our panda is a middle-aged male, physically active and independent. He is awake and will spend the day moving, eating and looking for a female panda.

12 noon   No sign of anything interesting to report within the past six hours. Midday means feeding time for our panda. He has stopped moving, needing a boost of energy to continue. Where is he going? The question we intend to answer. To recognise this subject, we have between the hours of 9 and 11, placed a large noisy bell around his neck along with a name tag to remember him by: *Wallis*. We are now monitoring Wallis' progress in a satellite van, complete with plasma TV screens and complex radio headphones. We don't expect you to understand. We are also using 'tree cams' and 'robo-panda-cam', this is a new piece of equipment supplied by National Geographic, a life-sized, fur textured robotic panda, who will stalk the subject, catching unique footage whilst blending in perfectly with the surroundings.

Lunchtime. The giant Vietnamese panda, (like all pandas) feeds stereotypically on canes of bamboo. These provide the panda with vital nutrients and sugar to give them energy. What for? The question we intend to answer. Look at him chewing away. Wallis will spend only half an hour lunching, before he is once again on the move.

Jack Langley (14)
Torpoint Community School, Torpoint

Tom The Toddler

This is the legend of Tom the Toddler.

Tom was two at the time he lost his precious gift. He loved that gift with all his heart and alas, it had been taken by an unknown person while Tom was sleeping. Tom was very suspicious of every person, but one in particular, the Evil One. While he was in this torturous time Tom could rely on one person Mummy the Fair Maiden. She was Tom's chief councillor and told him one or two bedtime stories. She told him of the Evil One coming in his room and taking the precious gift. Believing in a fair conclusion Mummy the Fair Maiden came up with another story of why this happened. But Tom was too excited by the fact he knew where his possession was and ran off.

Climbing over obstacles and crawling under others there was no stopping him. A hero on a perilous quest, with his blanket under one arm and teddy under the other. Fighting dragons and ogres, beasts and hounds. Racing up flights of stairs and jumping great heights he found it. Our hero crept quickly over the ground not making a sound. Holding his breath as he passed the Evil One he reached his quarry. Grasping it and holding it high, he stuffed it into his mouth, at last his dummy he had and so he fell asleep on the Evil One, his dad.

When brave Tom did arise he now had the greatest prize of his dummy. A great feat of bravery he had completed and an alliance he had created. As now he is friends with the Evil One, or now as he is called the Big One. 'All's well that ends well,' he said as he approached his advisor and gave her a kiss. 'Please take me to my bed and a fairy tale put into my head!'

And with that our hero leaves us to dream of a better world where the dummies flow freely.

Paul Creek (14)
Torpoint Community School, Torpoint

A Day In The Life Of A Prisoner

I woke up this morning to stale air in a compressed room, with rusty metal sink and toilet, and a rock-hard mattress, this is what I call home. This is all I deserve.

I am a prisoner here for the next five years because of ten minutes pure stupidity, which is what got me in the hellhole in the first place, I'd prefer not to talk about my past as there are few highlights that I can look back on.

I feel I have thrown my life away and let everybody down, but when I get out of here I am determined to prove to everyone I am a good person. Here in prison I have one thing to look forward to, which is the weekly visit I get, but it is still hard to enjoy with the guards constantly staring at you, monitoring your every movement.

The atmosphere here is like no other, murderous eyes everywhere, looking to do anything to relieve their misery. The screws are not much better, if they get bored they will need something to entertain themselves with, either by beating you to a pulp or your mate!

Josh Grant (14)
Torpoint Community School, Torpoint

A Day In The Life Of A Trench Soldier
(An extract)

Here I am, ten years on and I still remember that horrendous day like it was yesterday. I can still see the devastation and destruction everywhere. The sight of dead soldiers is scalded into my brain, never to be removed. I can still smell the reek of death and I can still taste the bitter resentment and hurt caused by just having to be there and see all those unspeakable things. They are memories that are not allowed to be forgotten.

It was early on the 17th August 1916. I had just crawled out of my lice-infested bed when the sound of the scrambling cat-like rats resounded through my head. They were scrambling around everywhere, feeding on the dead corpses sprawled across the ground. I had a sickening breakfast of stale bread and warm, dirty water, but it made no difference to me. Like I could eat anyway! Seeing my friends and fellow soldiers murdered and their hero bodies dumped into a hellhole kind of has that effect on you.

By 7am everybody was up and ready for action. I was placed on the dreaded machine guns and I hated it. We had all been warned earlier that day that the enemy was getting ready to attack and I didn't want to be on the front line.

Then it started. The shells started coming. They caused devastation. An unbelievable amount of damage was done and many men lost their lives. Body parts were scrambled everywhere and the screams and pleading of soldiers to be let home to see their precious families. The numbers of soldiers injured, dead or with shell shock just kept rising.

Louise Cordrey (14)
Torpoint Community School, Torpoint

Revenge On A Drake's Will

I was 13, I was coming back from the fields to find my entire home burnt to the ground. No sign of my family or friends, nothing. This is my life, now enjoy the story.

My name's Boar, I'm a Viking warrior from the Nordic realm, I never used to have to fight, but now I can't go one month without risking my life in some way, either in a fight with a drunk ork grunt or in running from a pack of hydras.

After my life was ruined I set off in search of the monster who murdered my family and set my home ablaze. I searched for two years and finally found the beast asleep in its cave. My sword stuck deep into its neck, but then I realised that this drake was only a child of two or three years old. This was not my demon, but I didn't care, I changed my hunt, widened my range, killing one drake wouldn't bring my family back, but killing more may save others from my fate.

It has now been 18 years since my family were killed and in that time forty-three drakes have been left dead by my sword. I stop in towns to get supplies and find short jobs or bounty hunts, my line of work doesn't exactly pay the bills, but I do get donations and offers of help, I take what I can but volunteers normally don't last longer than a month.

My latest job has been to hunt down a drake tamer named Thorn, he'd been setting drakes on the local villages, hopefully I'd find a few drake breeders the more the merrier I didn't care.

I tracked him down to the Barrier Mountain region according to the villagers he'd been seen heading out of the centre of the mountain region, a place known as The Blazing Heart.

It took me three weeks to track him down, but when I found him there wasn't exactly a lot left to bring back. The head had been ripped from the torso and the torso itself had been left half eaten, I didn't care, it just made the job easier. I took the head back with me to the town and collected the bounty. While I was there I picked up a tip on where a drake nest was and headed off. It would probably take me another two months to reach the nest but that's another story.

Dean Owen (14)
Torpoint Community School, Torpoint

Keen To Stay Green
(Based on a true story)

Midfield magician Akos Buzsacky has told Evening Sport that he wants to stay at Plymouth Argyle.

Akos has had his four month loan at Plymouth and it has been very successful. His club FC Porto have already had an offer for Akos from Plymouth but it has failed due to the asking price the club wanted. Akos is now in his home town in Hungary. He said, 'I'm spending my time with my family waiting for a phone call about my future, I would love to stay at Plymouth because I think the fans like me and it's a really great football team. Everything is great, but it's not my choice!'

Argyle's manager Bobby Williamson and chairman Paul Stapleton have both said that they want to sign him. Akos has made 15 appearances for Argyle after arriving from FC Porto in January. He has scored one for the club in a 1-0 home win for the Greens. Posters with messages saying, *Sign Him On,* at the last game of the season suggest that the fans do like him and would like him to stay at the club. The final score was a 0-0 draw with Leicester at Home Park. Akos said, 'I really enjoyed my time at Plymouth. I'm really impressed because it's a really nice club with really nice people. I came here in January and we got good and bad results, but we should move up in the championship which is what we wanted to happen, this is really good for the club's morale'. Akos is now awaiting for the news of his future at Plymouth, but everyone at the club would love him playing in the championship with Argyle.

His asking price was £350,000 (500,000 Euros) but hopefully FC Porto will lower the asking price, 'After all, no one likes to play B team football,' explained Akos.

Ben Surman (14)
Torpoint Community School, Torpoint

A Day In The Life Of A Rabbit In A Product Testing Facility

Do you know what it's like to get eyeliner in your eye? I do, I know too well! That was my first day at work, I was taken into a pitch-black room and I had to sit on a cold metal table in the middle of the room. The smell of decaying meat hung heavily in the air. Then the dim lights turned on giving me enough light to see round the room. In front of me stood a hunched, elderly man. My fear and confusion turned into relief, relief that I wasn't alone, but suddenly, from behind, another person grabbed me and held my eyes open, their hands were cold. Then came the eyeliner.

That was my first time of being in that room, but it wasn't my last. I've now been here for about a year and nearly every day I have had to test the new product. I'm 1307, that's what they call me, but my friends know me as Rabbit. I have made two good friends, Monkey is a good friend, he is in the cage to my left so we often talk. He has no fur due to a reaction caused by a shampoo product. To my right is Dog, he hates all humans, can you blame him? He also has many scars on his body, but he won't tell us how he got them. Monkey has been in here for about seven months and no one knows how long Dog has been in here as he was one of the first animals experimented on.

Cleo Summers (14)
Torpoint Community School, Torpoint

A Day In The Life Of A Soldier At Dunkirk

The cold rain poured rapidly on the diminutive beach, the dark, dingy clouds hovering over our heads. The flashing of the lightning blinding us as we waited patiently for our vessels to arrive. There's 300,000 cold, wet, muddy, wounded soldiers getting ready for another battle and the odds are totally against us and I'm ready to fight for my country.

Suddenly the rain started to pour more rapidly and the clouds were getting darker. The thunder was roaring louder and the sound of the thunderous Nazi tanks rumbled over the hills of the small village at Dunkirk. All I could see behind me was the crashing of the waves against the British and French ships storming ahead over the rampaging sea. I turned my head, but before I could turn the trembling sounds of the firing started. I snatched my gun, sprinted to the nearest ditch and dived into the dark, dingy, damp ditch. I climbed to the top, loaded my machine gun and started to fire at the Nazis. I wasn't aiming. I was hoping.

I kept checking to see how far the vessels were. I estimated roughly that they were about 20 miles out to sea. I picked myself out of the stinking ditch and ran to my best friend Steven Bekner and told him to run to the boats. He agreed with me, so we started to shuffle on our elbows and knees to the beach. I turned my head sharply and noticed that Steve wasn't there. 'Steve, are you all right? What's happened?'

Tom Payne (13)
Torpoint Community School, Torpoint

A Day In The Life Of A Cockleshell Hero

I woke up in my cabin to find a yellow envelope on the desk. I opened it, then read it eagerly, but I found that it was my mission: Destroy the German war vessel heading towards Britain.

I remembered the last time I did this: it was one year ago, my friend Major Timing and I were on a mission to destroy the German war vessel heading to America. We were going to canoe up in darkness to the vessel and plant the explosives on her hull. By the time we got out to the ship it was sheer darkness. All we knew was to follow the sound. We started to plant a ring of explosives, when we realised Major Timing was stuck on a rock and could not move. We had two minutes to get away. Timing bawled at me to go and to save myself. I tried to pull him off the rock but he was actually tied to the vessel. I paddled off; the ship sank with Timing tied on and I have never seen him since.

Two hours later I was setting up my canoe and getting ready for my journey to demolish the warship. All I had to do now was to stock up on supplies and to get my canoe into the unforgiving sea.

Three hours later I was in the sea, unable to see anything. All I had was the smell of smoke and the sound of the ship's engine. I thought, *if I destroy this ship it will be my last.*

The smell of smoke filled my lungs when the ship's lights came into sight. I commanded my squad to get into their positions. All five of us paddled towards the ship. I heard two of my team members capsize due to the waves the ship was generating.

When I reached her hull I made a careful ring of explosives. If I were to drop any then all of them would plunge towards the seabed. Done, I padded away from the ship. I was about 200 yards away when I heard the sound of her hull caving in. I saluted towards the privates and congratulated them on the completion of our mission.

The next day I was awarded a medal of appreciation and I retired.

Sam Hough (13)
Torpoint Community School, Torpoint

A Lost Child

I was 13 years old during the war. From 1933 to 1945, six million of my people died terrible deaths. Many were shot, some starved and most burnt in ovens and gas chambers. I was born in 1929, I think. My mother abandoned me and I was taken in by the Hacht family. They were good to me, they gave me a roof over my head, food and most importantly, love. We lived in Frankfurt until 1933 when we heard the Nazis began to persecute the Jews, so we moved to the Netherlands. This is a day in the life of 'a lost child'.

I woke up from a sudden boom. My heart felt like it was pounding faster than even a milli-second. It was the first of the bombings. I ran into my parents room.

'Mama, Papa, quick the Germans are here,' I cried fearfully. As Mama went to see to my sister I just stood there. It felt like my world was coming to an end. My mind went blank, I didn't know what to do or where to go. I wanted to curl up and think that it was all a dream.

'Wake up Marie, wake up!' I repeated in my head, but nothing seemed to make it go away. So all night long we crouched up under our kitchen table. Not knowing whether we would see the light of day or smell fresh air ever again.

The next morning we had to live life as normal. Get dressed, eat breakfast and go to school. My sister Anne was only 6 years old. Bless her heart, she was terrified of the bombs. She only just about understood, she always asked why. All I could say was everything is going to be all right. I didn't feel hungry at all that day. My stomach felt like it had been churned by fear. As I made my way to school, I could see the devastation that the Germans had done. At least five of our buildings had been brutally demolished. Our school was all right though. Which was a relief, but there was bad news to come.

Charlotte Goodacre (12)
Torpoint Community School, Torpoint

A Day In The Life Of A Victim Of Bullying

I knew today would be like any other. I couldn't stand it anymore; the same thing happening over and over again. A hit here and a thump there. Why was this happening to me? What had I done to deserve this?

There I was getting dressed when Mum called me for breakfast. I walked downstairs with my feet dragging behind me, but I couldn't eat anything. My stomach was in knots. What was going to happen to me today? Mum didn't know about it - only you do. I lazily packed my bag and put my shoes on.

There I was walking to school, nothing had happened yet. I'd got to the school gate and still nothing had happened. A smile lit my face as a wave of relief passed across my head. I knew that this was premature. But then as I walked through, there they were - right in front of me. I knew that it was too good to be true.

Why were they shouting? I was no different to them. Not richer or poorer, but this abuse five times a week.

It all started in September. I had moved here from South Africa, but now I wish we hadn't, just because my skin is a different colour that doesn't make me different, does it?

Chelsee Gill (13)
Torpoint Community School, Torpoint

A Day In The Life Of A Nurse In Pearl Harbour
(An extract)

December 7, 1941

When I woke this morning the sun was rising, a beautiful orange. Tiny, white, fluffy clouds littered the never ending blue sky. A cool breeze rustled through the tall, evergreen palm trees causing them to flap gently.

My duty at the hospital started at 7.35 in the morning. I had only been cleaning the ward for twenty minutes when Hell arrived on Earth. The atmosphere seemed to change and instead of joy and happiness, there was terror. The sky turned from a brilliant blue to a thick, heavy grey. I ran to the door and saw people screaming and running for cover. I saw mothers screaming for their children and friends screaming for each other.

The ever familiar sound of the enemy we so feared was edging nearer and nearer. Japanese bullets and shells dropped everywhere like pins and people dropped one after the other like flies, slaughtered by the enemy.

There were more of these monsters out at sea. Attacking each US naval vessel with as much ferocity as the first. With each hit, blasts of fluorescent orange smoke exploded into the air and then imploded into a dark, dismal grey. Bodies of dead sailors layered the black, oil water, which flared out in bursts of vibrant orange.

Within minutes, a surge of mutilated human bodies filled the partially clean ward. Blood poured from every vein, then dripped onto the floor. Bodies were being rushed in by the hundreds. Some on stretchers and some in people's arms.

Nicole Talbot (13)
Torpoint Community School, Torpoint

The End

Cheese can give you nightmares, but this is not a nightmare. I had a friend who loved cheese and ate it every day for lunch. He would do anything for it, even trade his life for it.

Once he had run out of cheese he would go and find a restaurant or supermarket that would sell him a kilo of cheese. Last year in this town they had no cheese at all and he had to go out of town to get some. He found a restaurant in Milbrook that he had never been to and ordered lots of cheese. Earlier he had told me about this place and told me to meet him there.

I never found it!

Forrest Kernan (12)
Torpoint Community School, Torpoint

Little Blue Riding Hood

You have all heard the story of Little Red Riding Hood. But what about her sister, Little Blue Riding Hood? She hates her sister for killing her best friend Mr Wolf and Red Riding Hood hates her because she shouts at their grandma.

'Hello sister,' said Blue, 'we meet in the woods for a final showdown, convenient.'

'Yes, where your mangled corpse is going to lay and rot,' said Red.

Blue quickly pulled her gun out from her belt and shot Red in the head.

'That was easy.' Then she went home and dyed the blue coat red.

Adam Stone (13)
Torpoint Community School, Torpoint

The Lady In Red

There was a lady who didn't have many memories or family left. She kept on dreaming about things. Until one day she was staring into mid-air, when she all of a sudden ran into the kitchen and grabbed a knife. She was screaming, 'Get out of my house, you abandoned me!'

Then she started to stab mid-air, well we thought it was mid-air but there was blood flying everywhere and she was covered in it. From that day forward everyone called her 'Lady in Red'.

Racheal Phelps (13)
Torpoint Community School, Torpoint

A Day In The Life Of A Child In Slave Labour
(An extract)

My day starts well before sunrise. My brother and I wash in the stream and share a bowl of rice and drink some water. I complain a great deal about my standard of life, but I am lucky enough to have a water source. I hold truckloads of sympathy for people who don't have a reliable source of water, but I certainly don't take it for granted. I have to often carry my younger brother to our allocated workplace because he is often too weak and feeble to walk himself.

It is now May and I have eaten two slices of meat this year, so it's understandable we feel so weak.

My contribution to this 'company' is that I stitch the flaps to the bladders of footballs. The only variation of my task is the colour of the flaps. The needles on our machines are blunt which makes it extremely tough to be accurate. But in almost a blackmail deal, if the balls are not *perfect* then we get punished, such punishments as being forced to use an even blunter needle resulting in loss of valuable wages, to getting beatings. As nearly all of us are gauntly thin and are so weak it knocks us to pieces being beaten. I have only been beaten once, but I felt like a crusty bit of crumbling bread. We may be weak physically, but mentally we are as strong as a piece of granite. All the torment we experience is something of amazement. It's a shame they don't have one of those world famous Record Breakers books in Algeria, because not many would disagree, all our names should be in big capital letters on the front page.

Michael Osborne (12)
Torpoint Community School, Torpoint

The Bloody Rope

'The party's at 9pm,' shouted Mel to Hayleigh who was directly in front of her.

'I'll be there,' Hayleigh sighed tiredly.

Mel was just getting ready when she heard knocking. She hurried downstairs because her boyfriend was coming to the party.

Crash!

A raging man had hit Mel over the head with a crowbar. Blood was pouring everywhere. Then the man hung her over the landing.

'Mel, Mel,' hammered Hayleigh knocking on the door.

Hayden said, 'The door's open.'

They stepped in to see Mel and the bloody rope …

Jade Walkden (13)
Torpoint Community School, Torpoint

The Boogey Man

There was an old couple driving down the motorway when a newsflash came over the radio.

'A crazed lunatic has escaped from a mental home'.

They drove through a tunnel, it was pitch-black. The man looked across at the passenger seat and saw his wife had gone. A van came beside him, the driver was pale white, pointing at the back seat. He looked behind and saw a man covered in blood with a knife. He looked back again and the man's world went black …

Luke Jones (13)
Torpoint Community School, Torpoint

The Graveyard Bet

A group of young girls were having a sleepover at Lilly's house one night. They were bored and decided to tell ghost stories.

It was Georgia's turn first. Suddenly Lilly had an idea, to play dares! Lilly dared Georgia to go to the graveyard opposite the house and stick a bit of wood in the ground to show that she had been there.

Ellen whispered to Jas, 'I wouldn't do that, it is a hell of a dark night!'

Georgia got up and stared out the window, it was pitch-black and the wind was howling! Georgia exclaimed, 'I don't want to go, it's too dark!'

Everyone apart from Ellen was then shouting, '*Chicken, chicken!*'

Georgia slipped on her jacket and shoes. Everybody went downstairs with her and Lilly opened the front door.

'Come straight back won't you?'

Georgia was off. An hour went by, surely she should have been back by now? They all slipped on their shoes and went to find her. Georgia was laid in the middle of the road. The wood was gone from her hand.

They entered the yard. The wood was in the graveyard. She had been there. On the way back she had been run over! She must have been so scared, she ran back without looking!

Lilly burst out crying so did the rest!

'It's all my fault!' cried Lilly.

Louise Bond (12)
Torpoint Community School, Torpoint

The Black Panther

Five girls were all practising for ten tours. They had been walking for so long they just had to sit down. In the corner of one girl's eyes was a black vision. The girl shouted, 'I feel dizzy.'
'Are you OK?' said everyone else.
'Yes, just a bit dizzy.'
They all carried on eating their lunch. Then all of a sudden they all started to hear noises like rustling and trees' leaves moving around!
'What?' said Jessica.
'Can you hear that?' said Lucy.
'*What?*' they all shouted.
'Where is Sophie?' said Jessica.
'Yes, where is she?' asked Lucy.
'Look!' shouted Maisy.
'Argh!' they all shouted.
Sophie was behind the boulder with her top ripped and blood dripping everywhere, with a big scratch!
'Who did this?' they all asked.

Chelsey Clarke (12)
Torpoint Community School, Torpoint

Hookey!

As Lisa finally put her 'Hen Night' top on and slipped into her shoes, she found a message on her phone. The message read, 'Don't forget to meet us all at Nick's house. Love Diana'.

Lisa replied with a happy smile, soon to be destroyed! She locked the door and started to walk down the road to Nick's house. Her feet soon started to ache so as the street was empty and starting to get dark she took her shoes off.

Lisa could hear someone walking behind with what sounded like flip-flops on. She turned around pretending to be playing with her hair. She couldn't quite tell if it was a boy or a girl, it was quite a short person, very skinny. Lisa took out her phone and tried to ring Diana, but her phone was switched off. As the person drew closer, Lisa grew scared. She turned fully round to find a hooked hand pierced into her *skull!*

Hannah Rosson (12)
Torpoint Community School, Torpoint

A Day In The Life Of Knight Poncy-Pants

19th December

I awoke this morning with a beautiful girl in my lovely bronzed arms. I didn't send for her, it must have been Father, he knows what a handsome young son like me needs. As I was showing her the door I caught a glimpse of myself in the mirror; it reminded me how utterly gorgeous I am.

I walked briskly in the fresh air down to the village, when I saw a beautiful, pure-white stallion stood in the clear water of the moat. It looked nearly as much of a strong hunky hunk that I am! I flicked back my hair and ran down in a manly way, and stopped a mere three feet away from it. I noticed he had a black star shape above his right eye and a sore-looking gash on his left front knee.

I held out a piece of grass from the bank, I felt very proud of myself, trying to touch a wild stallion is very brave. The horse gingerly sniffed my hand and suddenly reared up. I was so surprised I fell backwards onto the muddy bank and slid down. I was absolutely covered in the muddy gunge, eventually I clambered up (looking around first) and flicked the beast's nose gently. It looked at me with its big, black, twinkling, marble eyes and I fell in love. I stroked his soft muzzle and led him up to the castle grounds.

Firstly I took him to the doctors where he cleaned and bandaged the wound and then I took him to the blacksmiths where he got a brand new wardrobe full of different shoes. After that I took him to the royal horse groomers. When he came out looking stunningly sparkling, I remembered what I myself looked like and screamed a very high-pitched scream. I sped up to the castle with my clean horse.

When I had changed I collected my stallion from the stables and took him to meet my family. They all clapped and cheered when I told them my brave adventure, which included only a tad of improvisation. My silly little sister asked his name, I thought about it and asked her what she thought it should be and she said, 'Mr Fluffy-Bunny.'

I decided against it and named him *Spirit!*

Lucy Duncan (13)
Torpoint Community School, Torpoint

Forever Blank

The rain smothered the house in a fluid. The trees smashed into each other. A distant light could be seen. It was a house, in the middle of nowhere. Slates were hanging by a thread; the door looked shabby with a coating of filth layered on top. The name 'Hilltop' was positioned by the door.

'She told me to do it. She wanted me to. I was just doing what she said.'

She was sat in the corner of the single room; a picture of a boy was on the wall. The wallpaper was torn into shreds. The carpet had a distressed smell; it was as if a body had been left to rot.

'It's not as if it mattered, it ... it ... it was an accident, she didn't mean what she said.'

A silence came across the surroundings, not even the sound of the wind could be heard. The smell of death was still so close, it was so distinct, it had a part of the house.

The lady was creeping around the house; she stopped and glanced at the picture of a boy. A young, fresh face with glorious blond hair, cheeky grin and bright blue eyes, it looked like a perfect child. She turned the picture over and walked to the window, gazing outside. It was dead, nothing was moving and all was so still. The trees had frozen like icicles, the wind had gone silent.

'It's not right, why is it being like this? I know she wanted me to. I know I did it, I did it. But I want him back, but no I'm a b****, I can't.'

She lowered her head and stepped into the bathroom. The bathroom couldn't describe itself. Tiles chipped off with a huge layer of dirt and grit around the bath. The shower curtain had slashes in it, it was hanging by a couple of stitches. The sink was smothered in blood, razors were by the sink, packets of pills on the sink and scattered over the floor.

She looked into the mirror above the sink, her face was blank with no expression, her hair covered most of her face. Her eyes were red, drawn and bags had appeared underneath her eyes. She tried to look closer, the reflection wasn't of her face anymore, a tiny child was giving her his hand, tears dropped down from his face. It was the boy from the picture.

Words were trying to come out of his mouth, 'Mummy ... why, please no.'

She screamed in rage and swung at the mirror. It cracked and dropped into the sink. She sank onto the floor in desperation and unhappiness. A plea of hope. There was nothing she could do, he was gone and she had no one else. Her hand crept up onto the sink and she grabbed a piece of glass.

Pulling up her sleeves, her wrists were scarred; gashes all over, not a clean piece of flesh could be seen.

'It's the only way to ... to happiness. It's what makes me happy.'

She placed the glass over her wrist and slowly drew it across, time after time, slash after slash. A sigh of relief could be seen, her satisfaction had come through. The blood dripped onto the floor and she lay there ready for death.

Tom Willcocks (15)
Torpoint Community School, Torpoint

A Day In The Life Of A Light Bulb

One random, dull day I was made in a light bulb factory. Then I was tested, not with much care! But I didn't work. So they tested me again and again and again. Two days later I worked so I was sold to a school, a very dark and creepy school. Torpoint Community School, actually.

I looked around and around again. It was final, all I could see was a cardboard box. After a while I suffered from severe depression. Another month went on, I became claustrophobic! It was the worst feeling in the world. It was awful. After 322 days, 58 minutes and 12 seconds I was moved.

It was the most amazing feeling in the world! I didn't feel sick, I wasn't claustrophobic or depressed. It was the best day of my life. What happened, well ...

I was taken out of my box. The big wide world was my oyster! I was put in another cover. This one was clear. Long. It became dark 22 hours later. I was lonely. Then at about 8.55am thirty most amazing creatures came in shouting and screaming followed by one huge thing who called all the little angels, 'students'. I mean what's this all about? The students called this giant monstrosity 'Miss Lockett' or some called her 'teacher'!

Then someone switched me off. Absolutely disgraceful it is! Then on again. Then off, on, off, on, off, on, off, on, off, on, off, on. I guessed what was coming next - off and I was right. I guessed that on was next. But I was wrong. Darkness for the rest of my life. The day in the life of a light bulb - isn't it interesting!

Cali Fielding (15)
Torpoint Community School, Torpoint

Demented Child

Three years ago there were two 13-year-old boys who practically lived together. They were the best of mates. They went down by the harbour and had an argument over a girl at school and who she was going out with, (she was going out with them both).

Simon swung for Aaron but missed and all of a sudden there was thunder and lightning. Aaron hit Simon and he fell on a load of spikes on the ground and died. Ever since this happened, Aaron has felt guilty.

Three years to the day, Aaron walked down to the harbour and saw Simon's ghost. He pointed to Aaron and said, 'Prepare to experience the pain and loss I have, you ungrateful pig ...'

James Gibbs (13)
Torpoint Community School, Torpoint

The Graveyard Dare

There was a group of girls at the park at 11.00 in the evening and they were playing dare games. A girl called Claire was dared to go over to the graveyard across the road and dig a grave up after telling ghost stories!

'Hey guys, shall we play dares?' asked Robyn.

'Yeah, great idea. We'll use the stories to play,' explained Christina.

'I'm saying the dare first. I dare Claire to go into the woods and dig up a grave and if she chickens out, she'll be in for it. And believe me, she will!' said Jayne.

'Can't somebody come with me?' said Claire.

'No, no, no. You're gonna do it all by yourself!' they all shouted.

'Follow me down to the graveyard. I've got a spade for you to dig with!' said Jayne.

'Why are you making me do it?'

'Because you're the one who told the ghost story about the man coming out of his grave at 11.30 at night. It is now that time, so you're going to dig it up and see what happens from there ...'

Stephanie Tweedie (12)
Torpoint Community School, Torpoint

The Unexpected Birthday Treat

It was my best friend's birthday and she was 13. It was a stormy, cold day and she was meant to be having a pool party but not now. She was having a sleepover instead!

When I got round there, we started watching a really scary movie called 'The Ring'.

At 11.50 we all went to bed. I was the only one awake, everyone else was long gone. Suddenly there was a knock on the bedroom door and it creaked open. I felt a sharp tingle in the back of my neck. I was dead!

Alicia Keise (13)
Torpoint Community School, Torpoint

Life's A Witch

One day in medieval England, it was winter and the village was having its local witch trial. A young woman with black hair and dressed in rags was being chained onto a platform and a man in very expensive clothes spoke, 'Are you or are you not a witch?'

The lady looked up from her feet, with hate in her eyes . 'Yes I am.'

The people stood back a step.

Guards were called to take the witch to the lake. Most of the people followed the guards and the battered witch was hurled into the lake.

The wealthy man spoke again. 'This is where you die Witch. You see as the lake melts, you will drown. Isn't it brilliant?'

The witch spoke, 'As I die I will stay on this lake forever, dragging everyone into it. All because of your insolence.

200 years later.

'Hey, let's go on the lake ...'

Danielle Williams (13)
Torpoint Community School, Torpoint

The People Muncher

Dear Diary,
   Today I sat on my mahogany, old rocky chair. My arms are getting more and more weak every day. They are 76 years of age and aren't exactly brand new now. I turned the old metal switch up on the radio and sipped my cup of tea.
   'Listen in. Listen in!'
   I plugged my old frail ears to the speakers and turned the old metal switch higher until my old deaf ears could hear the voice clearly.
   'Eight school children and two teachers are trapped inside the mansion on top of Haunted Hill by creatures which have never been seen before. The children are diseased and we need to know everything about these things to keep the children alive. Please help if you know anything. Call 0800 988088. 0800 988088,' said the reporter clearly.
   I sat and looked at my leg, I remembered what happened with my other leg, it will happen to them. The people muncher is back . . .

Amy Maynard (12)
Torpoint Community School, Torpoint

Maniac In The Back Seat

A woman was driving to New York when her radio was interrupted by a special news bulletin. There was a maniac loose from a mental institution. She couldn't believe her ears. Suddenly she saw her car had low fuel. So she pulled over at the next fuel station. When she got there the man filled up her tank without looking in her car window.

The man walked up to the woman in the car and said. 'That will be $40 please.' He stopped and stared at something in the rear of the car.

'What is it?' she said and she turned around.

Click-click - a gun was held by the crazed maniac. He held it to her face.

'Don't shoot!' shouted the man and the woman.

Bang! blood everywhere and he did the same to the man and himself.

James Hough (13)
Torpoint Community School, Torpoint

The Hitchhiker II

A young lady was driving down a long and lonesome road one night, she saw something strange. She saw a frail old lady hobbling down the road. She stopped and offered the old woman a lift. The old woman accepted. As they were driving down the long road, they started to talk. They were talking about an escaped prisoner from Alcatraz. The escaped mass murderer was called Peter Andre.

As the old lady went to get something out of her handbag, the young lady saw the old lady's hands, they were big and hairy. The woman driver swerved and pretended to hit something so they both got out and had a look. The woman driver got back in the car and sped off into the dark.

Matthew Beadnall (13)
Torpoint Community School, Torpoint

The Graveyard Bet

One night a girl called Jemma was having a birthday sleepover with four friends.

'Mum, they're coming soon, where are the sleeping bags?'

'They're on top of my wardrobe!'

She went to the wardrobe and pulled out five sleeping bags when all of a sudden lots of paper fell down. She picked up the pieces of paper but one she picked up was a black piece of paper and it said on it *'You will die tonight!'*

She thought it was part of a game so she put it back and forgot about it. It was seven o'clock and the sleepover girls were arriving.

'Hey, let's tell ghost stories, the birthday girl should go first,' Kelly said, with enthusiasm.

'Last week a man was buried alive in the graveyard down the road; some say you can hear the scratching in the coffin, it's him trying to escape.'

'That's absolutely ridiculous,' Mina said, with a puzzled expression on her face.

'Prove it Jemma, I dare you to go to the graveyard and put a wooden stake in the ground to prove you were there!' Kelly said, with a stone-cold tone in her voice.

'Okay then, I will, as soon as my mum goes to sleep I'll do it.'

At 11 o'clock Jemma got ready to go to the graveyard.

'Are you sure you should do this Jemma? I'm sure Kelly will understand!' Kylie said, the scaredy-cat of the group.

'I have to do this.'

Half an hour after Jemma had left the girls heard a scream. They ran out the door calling Jemma's name, 'Jemma, Jemma, *Jemma!*'

They finally got to the graveyard, Jemma was lying by the man's grave. *She was dead!*

Carys Owen (12)
Torpoint Community School, Torpoint

Killer In The Back Seat

A man was taking a nice peaceful drive and then *boom!* the tyre popped. He got out to replace the tyre and whilst he was changing it, a man hopped into the back seat.

He carried on driving and then his exhaust fell off, so he went to a nearby garage. The mechanic stepped up to the car, grabbed the man, tried to pull him out of the car, but the man drove away and the mechanic finally shouted, 'There's a killer in the back seat!' and then blood squirted on the window.

Alex Bird (12)
Torpoint Community School, Torpoint

The Man-Eating Cheese

Most cheeses taste nice but this cheese doesn't taste nice and doesn't get eaten because no one likes the look of this cheese, it's green and smells like rotting bodies. This cheese is special, it eats people at 1 o'clock on Sundays or any other time or day. It's called Edam.

One Sunday at twelve o'clock a 7-year-old boy got sent down to the shops to get some cheese. He got to the dairy place and pointed towards the Edam cheese. He got the cheese, paid and walked out. It took him ten minutes to get home, he made a sandwich and his mum shouted, 'Get in the bath!' He was in there for 40 minutes and then he got dried and ate the sandwich.

The clock ticked away to 1 o'clock, the cheese came alive and … bit his ear off and blood spurted everywhere. He screamed …

Scott Redding (13)
Torpoint Community School, Torpoint

The Hole

Claire had come home from work when she heard her Italian Spinone, Jacob was barking frantically. She ran inside to find her Labrador, Gemma, lying on the floor barely breathing. She grabbed her and rushed her to the vet's, leaving Jacob at home.

The vet said she had something stuck in her throat and that she needed an operation immediately.

Shaken, Claire trundled back to her car and drove home. Jacob was waiting for her, barking to go outside. Claire thought, *it's such a nice day, why don't I do some gardening?* As she went outside she found Jacob sniffing and yelping about something.

Claire realised that a year ago that day, when she had first moved to the house a murder had been committed and they had never found the body.

Nice anniversary date, Claire thought. She walked over to Jacob to see what he was excited about and found a 6 foot hole, she peered down into the bottom of it and found someone staring back at her.

'Argh!' Claire screamed and ran inside and phoned the police.

While the police searched she stayed inside looking out into her garden.

The police finally finished and told Claire that the body was of Heather Clansey who was the girl that had been murdered a year before and an eye wasn't there and that was it. That was when the phone rang. The vet had operated and Gemma was fine, what was causing the loss of breath was an eye lodged in Gemma's throat.

Alice Edlin (12)
Torpoint Community School, Torpoint

Anonymous
(An extract)

I was crouched under the free soup table again. No family left, no warmth left in me, no love left in me and most importantly no life left in me. Four months I had been waiting for the trip of my life and now it had come I didn't know if I wanted to go. It was a big risk, but was it a risk I was willing to take? There were other people in this so-called campsite but they were different to me, they had family. Down at the end of the big wall were three families. There was the Indian father, Pundarik and the mother, Parul, and their two sons Amar and Amal. Then there were the Russians, Dmitri and Inna. The last family had one member and he was Chinese. His name was Dèng Xiāopíng. I had come all the way from Egypt to get to the so-called Promised Land, Plymouth. Everyone but myself was talking about Plymouth, Plymouth this and Plymouth that.

I could hear a low-pitched roar in the background. The hairs stood up on the back of my neck. Everyone ran over to the harbour. I was scared. All on my own. I ran with everyone else. Not knowing where I was being led to. The lorries were coming into the lanes. I had done this so many times before, but I was still scared that this time the outcome may not be the same as before. I made my approach as I usually did. They quickly opened the door and jumped in. I ran as fast as I could at the lorries without stopping for anything. I tried to open the lorry door. It was locked. All the other families were jumping into the back of their lorries and I was stuck outside. I was stiff unlike everything else, even the leaves were dancing on end. I stood frozen. All of a sudden, out of nowhere, there were three white people jumping into the lorry in front of me.

Benjamin Applegate (12)
Torpoint Community School, Torpoint

A Day In The Life Of A Band

There he was. Johnny Litch, formerly known as Jonosatis Saslitchas from Athens. He was the only child of the wealthy couple of Charistaes and Menlitov. At the age of four, he moved to England as his father had a job in London.

On a very sunny day in June, he and his band, Battle, were in their tour bus as they were touring the UK. His band consisted of Ronny Ashburn, John Lucas, Paul Jerke and Roger 'Fraggy' Fragg.

They were all looking forward to the next day as Live Aid was being shown live on TV. They were hoping to be performing on the day to remember but it wasn't to be.

Whilst bringing in the letters from fans they had an extraordinary posh envelope. Johnny opened this to find a lengthy letter. At first he couldn't believe it until it had sunk in. He was invited to perform at Live Aid at Wembley. Maybe a band pulled out or couldn't make it, or was it just a last minute invite?

Luckily, they didn't have to perform for their electrifying tour. Johnny told the rest of the band, they were so excited, they decided to go to bed early, not just to pass time, but also to get rest.

Louis Ryan (13)
Torpoint Community School, Torpoint

Red Beach
(A story of D-Day)

'Men, only two more minutes till we get ashore,' that was the last time the colonel spoke to us. We landed ashore and within seconds most of the people in my landing craft were killed.

I ran towards the sand mounds and hid to stay safe, then I saw him, he was so young, I shouted to him to get down but he was too slow, he got hit; I had to sit there and watch him die. I crawled towards him and took his dog tags, his name was Jeremy Delle, he was 16 and from Barnsley. I took the remaining bullets from his rifle, I scouted around for some more ammo but found something better, I found grenades, one had already been used but it was OK.

I started shooting but it was so hard to concentrate with all the screams of men dying behind me. The smell of death shot up my nose and singed my hairs, it was horrible, everyone was dying, it was so upsetting.

I remembered the last thing my father had said to me about coming here, he said that if I ever was in a position that I couldn't get out of I should get my knife and take it to my throat but only in extreme cases, I nearly did but then I remembered my family back home and I just couldn't do it.

I carried on shooting, a Nazi tank rolled close by, I threw a grenade and hit! Shrapnel flew through the air like trash caught in the wind.

Chris Waterfield (12)
Torpoint Community School, Torpoint

A Day In The Life Of An Aramanthian Dragon Slayer
(An extract)

The shadow of a giant, dark, winged beast swooped above the city of Aramanth. It descended and swung a clawed arm at a house, it crumbled to the ground. The creature roared with such ferocity the huge stone walls around the city shook. A woman sitting down on a street corner shrieked as the creature lunged at her, the sharp teeth ripped right through her flesh, she died instantly.

I awoke suddenly, I'd been getting these nightmares for the past week. I'm Coram and I'm a dragon slayer, I kill dragons for money, a lot of money. These nightmares have all been about dragons attacking my home city, Aramanth. I know this one means something but what?

I just get on with my usual or, you may call it unusual, life.

I clambered out of bed; I pulled on my leather tunic, grabbed my boots and stepped into the not so busy street.

'I saw it, it took Mrs Mackey three streets down, it came last night!'
'What came?' I questioned him.
'A dragon!' was the reply.

That evening I prepared, I heaved on my shiny steel armour, grabbed my bow, my quiver full of arrows, my shield, my long sword, my broadsword and my throwing knives. I took up my spear, hopped onto my horse, clipped on my cape and rode into the night towards the gatehouse.

James Bevan (13)
Torpoint Community School, Torpoint

A Day In The Life Of A Rock Star
(An extract)

God, I'm so tired. 3 hours sleep. But then again that's like a coma compared to how much sleep I had in the whole of last week. Going to bed at four in the morning, waking up at half-past. Touring is a joke. No family except 'bandmates'. But it seems like they're becoming my 'band-enemies' the way they were acting. Last night Pete, our bassist, drank a bottle of our friend Jack Daniels before the show. Needless to say, he played like crap and looked a right fool trying to start the gig jumping off his amp. Funny when, during a moment of slight soberness, he realised his amp was about 15 foot tall. He just stood in front of the amp, feedback piercing our (and the crowd's) ears, looking totally gormless before a crowd of thousands. I told myself, this is the last straw. Just like the night before that, the day before that and the afternoon two days before that.

Every day is the same. Pete is still asleep. Lucky. Wish I'd drunk a whole bottle of JD and got a concussion falling off my amp, maybe I'd get some more sleep.

Have you ever seen the film 'This is Spinal Tap'? Well basically, it's a pretend documentary about a band on tour and everything possible goes wrong. I went to see that at the cinema while having a rare moment off the tour bus, and I was, well, there isn't a word for it. I didn't know whether to laugh or just sit there working out how they managed to sneak film cameras into our interviews and onto our tour bus. It was so much like our band.

Will Bennett (13)
Torpoint Community School, Torpoint

Death

Death and misery had forsaken the once green and peaceful lands. The soothing scents of graceful flowers and the chattering bird calls which had filled the breezy air had been lost to the ages. War had come and could not be persuaded to leave. A looming shadow was passing, a dark menace lingering, just beyond the borders of the great land. A predator waiting to strike. But the vast ground was not unprotected.

The Fairinia were a proud and peaceful race, their love for the land was a gift to all others, even those who they fought bitter wars with were thankful.

They delighted in song and thrived in the making of towers, carved of marble and lined with silver, they glittered, in the fiery sun and glowed under the wrath of the dying moon.

They wore long blue gowns and their golden hair rested softly on their faces. And upon their flag, a symbol of their unique freedom, a blue dove.

But for them, the end was near. A great army of Treacherous Redcaps, Ruthless Konems and Towering Grogs came marching to the barren plains of Muilirnon. At three hours from sunrise, they halted. For upon the mound of Talorfin stood a small cluster of brave Fairinia. They were unarmed. As the filthy invaders stared, a song came from the hillock.

'The waves on the sea are foaming white, from the dawn of day, to the break of night and upon the land we shall stand tall, the loyal soldiers of the Fairinial.'

Adam Curtin (13)
Torpoint Community School, Torpoint

Are We Invisible?

'We are invisible.'

Hi my name is Emma. I have a mum, dad and a sister called Nat. Nat and I are twins, not identical though and I'm glad of that, I don't want her to have my good looks. Anyway let's get on with the story. It starts like this ...

I was sat in my room with my sister, playing Monopoly. The wind howled and the puddles grew. The water from our faces was drying as the warm breeze floated through the air from the radiator, we had just taken our dog out for a stroll, his name is Spot and he has a muddy-looking patch over his eye, he is so cute. Anyway where was I? Oh, yes I remember. As we were shouting at each other over whose turn it was Dad came thudding up the stairs carrying two huge cardboard boxes. He strolled into my room as though we were not there and started emptying my cupboard of all my games and animal books. Questioning what he was doing I stood up, he didn't say, 'Oh sorry dear, didn't realise you were in here' or 'Your mum and I have something to tell you', no he just stood and stared at me wishing that I didn't exist. Nat asked him again and he replied with, 'We're moving!' He said it to us as though we were stupid.

'What? ... How? ... When? ... Why? ...' A load of questions came steaming out of my mouth all squashing together as they hit the air. He didn't understand me, just looked and stared; he then picked up the bare box and walked across the room to my dressing table.

When the boxes were full and he had taken them downstairs. Nat burst out crying, I could see the blank expression on her face when Dad uttered the words that we thought we would never hear. Dad came thudding back up the stairs except he didn't come into my room. Horror spread across Natalie's face, she jumped up and swung the door open which made a gaping hole in the middle of the wall, a blood-curdling scream shot out of her mouth seeing her door wide open.

When I peeled open my eyes from all the pain from my ears to my toes, I darted into her room and found her taking out her belongings as Dad put them in. He didn't notice until he had turned round and saw all the mess now spread across the pink carpet. Grabbing us by the collar he pulled us downstairs and barricaded us into the shoe cupboard.

We hardly said a word in there. I felt like I had been eaten whole. It was dark, damp, very cramped and stunk of rotten cheese. I could hear Nat snivelling in the corner with a slight hiccup every now and again, with the click of her heels as though she wished they were 'Dorothy' heels so that she could get away from this horrible place and live in bliss for the rest of her life.

Gemma Viant (15)
Torpoint Community School, Torpoint

The Day In The Life Of Sebastian

Sebastian wakes up at 7am every weekday morning to go to work at a local milk factory.

It is Wednesday the 3rd of August 1981. Sebastian wakes up at 7am as usual and then he gets dressed, has a wash and some breakfast, watches a bit of TV, picks up his car keys, leaves his house for 8am then drives to work at the factory for 8.30am.

When he gets into work and puts his overalls on, gloves and hat then he heads off to his machine that he has been working on for the past three years. He knows how it all works. He sets up his machine as always, like he does five days a week and eight hours a day. His job is to get the old milk bottles washed and dried and to make sure they are clean without a spec of dirt.

Sebastian has been there cleaning and rinsing now for four hours. Sebastian takes a break at one o'clock for his lunch where he goes down to the café for a fried breakfast with a cup of tea and he reads the newspaper then heads off back to work for two o'clock. He then goes through the same procedure by putting his overalls and gloves with his hat on then goes to his machine and switches it on and he gets cleaning and rinsing, then he carries on doing that till five o'clock.

Sebastian finishes work and picks up his car keys and heads off to the kebab shop for a kebab, goes home grabs a can, switches the TV on, has a drink and eats his kebab and relaxes for the rest of the night.

Mark Floyd (15)
Torpoint Community School, Torpoint

My Short Story
(Inspired by the film 'Big' starring Tom Hanks)

It was morning at home. The glistening sun was rising with pride, the chattering birds were singing a song, the grass smelt fresh and the dewdrops twinkled like stars in the sky. I thought it was too good to be true. It was. I was right. It had come true.

Rushing, I tripped over as I shot downstairs. I crashed violently into the ruby shagpile my mother prized so highly. The thunderous noise must have startled her as she came running to see what had happened. She screamed violently and to my surprise started to hit me. Telling me to get out of the house or else she would ring the police. I repeatedly said, 'Mum stop it's me. Me, John; your son.' She just kept firing blows at me and repeatedly screaming, 'Get out, get out!' and 'What have you done with my son?' With some force she aggressively pushed me out the door. She had chucked her own son out. I wish I never made that stupid wish now. I'm stuck like this forever. I'm going to be 12 tomorrow but this stupid wish has made me 30. I want to be me again. Just a regular 11-year-old boy with a home and a loving mum.

I don't know how I'm going to tell my mates. I only saw them last night and everything was fine but now look at me. A 30-year-old man. Spiky, dark hair, 6ft tall, brown hazelnut eyes and that's just for starters. My body feels all tingly. It's as though I'm in someone else's shoes. It's not that that worries me, it's just ... it's just, people will think that I'm stupid. What I mean is that I have a mind of an 11-year-old but the looks and body of a 30-year-old. I've tried to look on the bright side, at least now I can go to the pub and have a stiff drink.

Sarah Killingsworth (14)
Torpoint Community School, Torpoint

A Day In The Life Of George
(Inspired by 'Of Mice and Men' by John Steinbeck)

When I look back on this day, I will probably remember it for the rest of my life. This is the day my association with Lennie finally ended.

It started just like any other day; I got up from my straw-based bed at 6am, tired from the previous day working. When everyone else had got up we went out onto the ranch and started our daily routine of bucking barley. It is hard but you get used to it. I looked around for Lennie but he was nowhere to be found; he was probably petting his pups.

Then something strange happened, Candy came running towards us, shouting. I couldn't quite catch what he was saying, but the rest of the guys started running to the barn, so I followed them. I was full of worry as I knew Lennie would be in the barn. Once inside we were all shocked as we saw Curley's wife lying there, but I could not find Lennie anywhere. I knew, as everyone else did, that it was Lennie who had killed her.

They all set out to kill him but I needed to find him before they did. I remembered what I'd told him that if he got in trouble; go hide in the shrubs.

Matt Barrett (14)
Torquay Boys' Grammar School, Torquay

A Day In The Life Of George

(Inspired by 'Of Mice and Men' by John Steinbeck)

George awoke to the stink of the bunkhouse. He had been woken by the intense orange sunlight streaming through the small pane of glass that Slim had persisted in calling a window.

'This bunkhouse stinks, I'm glad that dog's gone though, and we can get the Negro to clean the place now without it smelling straight after. I'm gunna go outside cos it really does stink in here.'

George exited the bunkhouse and sat on the step outside contemplating his life and looking at his breath in the fresh morning air.

'I like being here, we got all we need, it's like a big family. I got all I need here; food, shelter, friends and a pack o' cards. I heard Lennie get up this mornin', he's so clumsy he tripped on the end of my bed. I bet he's in with those pups again; he'd better not kill any o' them like he does those mice. Lennie ain't got no family so I look after him like he were. Better get workin' now I'm up, might as well get some barley bucked. Maybe I can bunk off early.'

George started to move slowly around the yard being careful not to make much noise. Lennie was in the barn, George got him up an' they went to work together.

Shaun Cockman (14)
Torquay Boys' Grammar School, Torquay

I Bring News

Once Qualis had entered the secret city of the Wilden elves he would be safe. The skilled archers would bring down the ogres effortlessly. The only problem was its position. Where was it? He would have to keep running until he reached the city. He could not do that. The ogres had been running for a shorter amount of time. They would catch up with him. He could not even begin to imagine what they would do ...

Whoosh! A fusillade of arrows shot out of the surrounding trees and undergrowth. Heavy, sharp arrows thudded into the ogres. The points pierced the thick hides. The ogres roared defiantly as they crashed to the ground, making even more noise than their kin did as they continued to charge through the thick forest. Another volley of shots crashed into the advancing ogres. At last Qualis saw his rescuers. They had nocked their arrows, preparing to loose yet more steel-fanged death upon the ntruders. They continued to fire until the entire ogre patrol was dead or had fled. Then a brown-skinned Wilden elf stepped out of the foliage. He kneeled and the rest of the scouts followed suit.

'Prince Qualisilvan,' the leader raised his head, 'I am honoured.'

'Take me to Kiliar,' ordered Qualis imperiously. 'I bring an important message.'

'Your Majesty,' stated the golden-haired leader, 'a lot has happened since you last graced this place with your footsteps.'

Ben Howitt (11)
Torquay Boys' Grammar School, Torquay

A Ninja's Honour

One dark, misty night, a lurking shadow fell over Main Street. The bewildering yet strangely familiar figure sat at the peak of a high building, only then to gracefully leap to another building then another.

Then, abseiling down to the floor, reaching the subway station, he landed. Walking slowly towards his target, and calmly drawing out a curved sword, he struck him down.

Leaping and twirling in the air, the now exposed red ninja, sliced down many more. Driven insane by the loss of his father, the ninja stabbed and pummelled more people. Reaching a man he knew would be there (the murderer himself) he leapt and took him to the floor.

With a powerful, so powerful, hit through the man's neck, he finished the rampage. Disappearing into the shadows, he vanished into the night.

Ben Sebastian (12)
Torquay Boys' Grammar School, Torquay

The Soul Snatcher

It's so horrible! I felt so cold and so alone on that dark, treacherous night. The wind was whispering in my ear, eerily, it said it again in a death-like drone, look behind, in a trance-like movement I turned. I felt icy breath along with a bone-like hand on my shoulder. I spun around, I wanted to scream, but something stopped me. I think it was then I met the eyes of my attacker, so hollow, so dark, he looked like a ghost, but like no other. Half of him seemed dead and the other half alive.

I sensed I was going to die! Suddenly, instinctively, my hand reached to grab a steel pole, as the pole left the ground, I stabbed the creature on both sides, life and death. An amazing scene was happening. The beast tried to change.

Life turned to death, death turned to life, but it was not working, I could barely watch as the creature rose up and started to shake violently. Suddenly it clicked, the creature was going to blow up! I expected to hear a loud bang, instead I heard a loud excruciating pain and such anger.

I looked up, instead of blood and guts there was a dark cloud of dust, like a dark hole in space, where no light can shine, but! dancing in the air, spreading far and wide, were dancing little balls of light ... they could only be lost *souls!*

Matthew Derbyshire (11)
Torquay Boys' Grammar School, Torquay

The Bear Clan's And Viper Clan's War

Claw grabbed his axe and shoved on his ox hide armour and his bear skin cape with the stuffed bear head to protect his own head.

Suddenly there was a giant boom and he knew that the Viper Clan's warriors had started ramming the gate with a battering ram.

He rushed towards the battlements, all the townsfolk were milling around the gate to the main structure of the castle, fighting to get themselves and their families to relative safety.

Claw climbed the steps to the battlements at breakneck speed, he heard the whistle of arrows and looked over the edge.

There were the Viper Clan with their dark armour and hair, and their pale, pale skin.

They were swarming like ants up the battlements pulling themselves up with ropes as the archers desperately tried to keep them at bay.

As a Viper warrior reached the top of the wall it saw Claw and charged at him with a horrible blood-curdling scream, sword raised ready to strike …

David Gabb (12)
Torquay Boys' Grammar School, Torquay

The Shortest Horror Story Ever Written

I am now going to tell you the story of my life. At the beginning I had an awful childhood. My parents didn't treat me with any respect at all. Great times I had in my teenage years as I achieved a great bond with my father. Other than this, my childhood days are over. I now do a dangerous job which I am not to speak of, I have to stay undetected. Never have I been seen or heard. Good and bad things I have done in the past 20 years. Then I heard news that broke my heart. Over the mountains where my parents' house was, you killed my father and mother.

'Killed' and 'dead' were the only two words in my mind at the time. I wasn't just going to let this get past me. Letting someone do such a thing without being punished would be a deed I couldn't cope with. 'Livid' was the only word to describe me. You are going to pay. Obviously you should watch every step you take because I might be there to pounce very soon. Unnoticeably soon!

Now go back through the last passage of writing starting with the first sentence and put the first letter of the first word in each sentence together. It'll spell out a sentence in which shivers will travel up your spine. Just remember my name 'Bubby Stalone'. It will haunt you for many years to come …

James Chatterton (12)
Torquay Boys' Grammar School, Torquay

Condemned

I lay there shaking like a leaf and sweating like I had had a nightmare. My eyes were closed and my heart was beating like a drum.

My teeth were chattering and I had bitten my nails to the extent that the top of my fingers and thumbs had drawn blood. Was this life or death? It didn't matter anymore.

I realised I hadn't breathed for a long time so I took a deep breath. All around me was cold and probably wet but I daren't open my eyes to check.

I have no last words or wills; I want nothing, there is nothing left. Hope is lost and my pride is but an inch from extinction.

I have lost the will to live and gained absolute fear of death. I need a rest, drowsiness is surrounding me and I feel like I am fading into thin air without a trace of my existence or a mark of a reputation.

Within a few minutes Hell will take my soul and the ground will take my bones and body. It is just a matter of seconds before I die, along with my peace and joy.

Who says everyone is equal? This is most definitely only happening to me, it's not fair. I am beyond sad, I'm petrified, I'm morose, I'm an infinite number of emotions at once and I'm tired of it being this way.

Jack Lang (12)
Torquay Boys' Grammar School, Torquay

The Fire

The fire was burning, high in the moonlight, the whole of the little, wooden town was ablaze. The nearby forest was the only shelter for miles around and even that was aflame. So how did this happen, you ask? Let's travel back a few hours and see, shall we … ?

Zak and his family were eating comfortably by the fire when they heard the thunder of hooves and the crackle of torches outside.

'Hide quickly!' his father whispered.

He crept over to the cupboard, a floorboard creaked, the horses stopped and their riders muttered something. He hid in the cupboard, the door groaned. *Thump! Thump!* Something or someone was hammering on the front door with a stick or something.

The door fell inwards and a cloaked figure entered the small, wooden hut Zak called home. He or it said nothing but dropped the torch it was carrying onto the wooden beams that held up the hut. It toppled down and the family tried to flee, but the thing, with one sweep of its torch, utterly annihilated all of them, except Zak who was safe in the last remaining structure.

The thing walked, or glided, onto its mount and rode away into the night, back to its master …

Ethan Luke (12)
Torquay Boys' Grammar School, Torquay

The Forgotten Village

The Survivor

I awoke with the hot sun beaming down on me through the cracks in the trees. I felt an aching on my forehead and, as I ran my finger along it, I could feel a huge lump. Then I remembered, yes that was it, I had gone out to fetch fruit for my family. It was getting dark so I thought that I better get back so I ran, hit a tree and then ... nothing. I must have been knocked out or something, as when I was collecting fruit it was summer and I had now awoken half buried in leaves and all the trees were empty of their leaves. I started to panic and wondered if I had been in a coma for years or if it was next season, but I was confused and did not know what to believe.

Shaking, I got to my feet and set off in the direction that I thought was home. I seemed to have been walking around in circles for hours when eventually I found a trace of what appeared to be the path leading up to the village.

I began to tremble as I looked ahead of me up this once new path. Just days before I left the village to collect fruit, this path was newly laid. I know for a fact that paths last a good amount of years and I was now certain that I had been gone for years. I looked over the hills and saw my village in ruins!

Barcley Spicer-Jenkins (11)
Torquay Boys' Grammar School, Torquay

Burnt Face Man Vs The Worm

It was an average day, chasing after villains, stopping them when this one guy came along. He called himself 'The Worm'. He was a quick worm but still no match for me, Burnt Face Man. I'm called this because my face is burnt but I don't know how.

OK so this guy came along, stole some expensive stuff and now he's a criminal mastermind trying to take over the world and it's my job to stop him.

Ring! Ring!

'Hello,' I said as I picked up the phone.

'Hello Burnt Face Man, we've just got word that The Worm is based down at the harbour in the big warehouse,' said the policeman.

'OK, I'm on my way.'

I got my cape and my suit on, and then jumped out of the window and flew down to the harbour.

I smashed through the warehouse doors.

'Well hello, we meet again!' said The Worm.

'Yes and this will be the last time,' I said, trying to sound heroic.

Suddenly The Worm shot at me, but I, with quick thinking, decided to stop it with my laser eyes, then I remembered I didn't have that power. I flew around in circles as The Worm shot again and again. Then I dived on him and with a struggle cuffed his wrists together.

'I've got you now,' I said as The Worm entered my cell.

'I'll get you someday, this isn't the end.'

Craig Murch (12)
Torquay Boys' Grammar School, Torquay

The Dark Knights

They were riding over the horizon, silhouetted against the sky by the setting orange sun. As the night came, the Dark Knights drove on, clad in their dark leather armour and their dark iron axes hanging loosely on their jet-black horses.

The tribe called The Storn were waiting at the top of their settlement. Even as they saw The Dark Knights coming and could hear the Death Angel whispering in their ear they still stood their ground and prepared to die.

The night was fresh and the moon shone out. It was a full moon, in the distance a wolf howled and an owl hooted and flew out of a tree in the nearby woods.

The deep, clear war horn of The Dark Knights rang out in the night and echoed in the nearby woods. The Dark Knights were closing in now, so close that the peoples of The Storn could hear the dull thud of horses' hooves on the stony ground.

The rain started pouring and a clap of thunder illuminated the scene for a second, but in that second what The Storn saw was enough to strike terror in even the bravest man's heart; a huge mass of strong, muscular horses with large men in control of them. The light of the moon illuminated the froth flying from their mouths. As The Dark Knights closed in The Storn knew they were in trouble.

Joe Arnold (12)
Torquay Boys' Grammar School, Torquay

Unidentified Body Found
(Inspired by 'Of Mice and Men' by John Steinbeck)

A body has been discovered on Tyler Ranch yesterday afternoon. The dead woman has not been named, although the latest rumours coming from the ranch suggest that it is the body of Curley's wife. Curley, who is the son of the boss of Tyler Ranch, has been called in for questioning but gave us this statement.

'That big blundering idiot Lennie done it! I'm gonna kill him myself!' he yelled as he was escorted to the police car.

The police have launched a manhunt for Lennie Small, who is described as tall and strong with a mental age of seven. He is also reported to be armed. Because of this, the public have been advised not to approach him aggressively.

A post-mortem examination has concluded that the woman died after her neck was broken. Lennie Small is regarded as the prime suspect because of his inability to control his strength. According to close friend and carer George Milton, this isn't the first time his lack of intelligence has got him into trouble.

'Yeah, we was workin' on a ranch in Weed, and we had to get outta there quick when he got into trouble for stroking this girl's dress. We had to hide in a damn irrigation ditch', Milton told us before walking off towards the woods.

It is unclear of the exact location of Small, but he can't hide forever. According to reports Curley is soon to be released on bail. This means that he is not a main suspect.

Tim McLennan (14)
Torquay Boys' Grammar School, Torquay

A Day In The Life Of Candy
(Inspired by 'Of Mice and Men' by John Steinbeck)

I woke up yesterday morning and went to work. It was just like every other day, cleaning up rubbish, as boring as normal. The pay isn't even very good! But it's the only job I can get with my one hand.

After my morning's work I went straight to the canteen for lunch, it was Friday so it was tomato soup. I usually have to queue up for ages because all the young workers at the ranch just push in front of me. It's like I'm not there.

When I'd got my food, I went and sat down and had my soup. Whenever I sit down on the chairs I just wish they would fix them or at least clean the tables. The place is a mess!

After I'd finished my soup I went straight to work. The sun was out and it was the hottest time of the day. I always get sunburnt, even if I stay in the shade. I carried on with my cleaning until I had finished and then went back to the bunkhouse. Everyone was there, gambling away just like every Friday night. Then Carlson came in, stressed out, and he had to take it all out on my dog.

He said my dog smelt and he was no use to me. He was going to shoot him! I pleaded for his life but he just wouldn't listen. I had to give in, but now I wish I hadn't. If he had to be shot I would have done it.

Kai Feller (13)
Torquay Boys' Grammar School, Torquay

Murder In Soledad
(Inspired by 'Of Mice and Men' by John Steinbeck)

Late last night Sandra Field was found dead at the Tyler Ranch. Police are treating it as murder.

Police are investigating the murder of Sandra Field. There are a number of suspects which include all of the workers on Tyler Ranch.

Many interviews are being carried out to try and get to the bottom of what so far seems to be one of the most mind boggling murder mysteries of our time.

The interviews have not uncovered much of what happened on the night of the murder. So far all of the workers have said the same thing. 'Well I was playing horseshoes at the time of the murder', said John Sampson (Whit). This seems to be the common answer to all of the questions asked by the police detectives. An interesting fact was uncovered during an interview with Simon Wills, also known as Candy, one of the workers on the ranch, he said, 'We were all playing horseshoes at the time of the murder. But the only person that wasn't was Lennie Small'. Police have classed Lennie Small as one of the prime suspects due to this new information.

The whereabouts of Lennie Small is unknown at this time. He is said to be armed and dangerous. Posters of what he looks like have been placed all around Soledad to keep the general public safe from who is said to be the killer of Sandra Field. Any new information would be very useful to police investigators. If you have any could you contact the nearest police station.

Max Russell (14)
Torquay Boys' Grammar School, Torquay

The Soledad Post

(Inspired by 'Of Mice and Men' by John Steinbeck)

Yesterday evening the deaths of Mrs Curley Carlson (24) and work hand Lennie Small at the nearby Tyler Ranch are believed to be connected.

Detectives are treating the deaths as 'mysterious and suspicious'. One man, another workhand at the ranch and friend of the dead man George Milton, has been detained by police and is currently being questioned regarding the events of yesterday morning.

His involvement in this case is apparent through his finding of both bodies and possession of a pistol at the site of Lennie Small's death. It is currently thought that Mrs Carlson was talking to Lennie in the Carlson's barn on Tyler Ranch, when an incident occurred which resulted in the snapping of the deceased Mrs Carlson's neck.

With the deaths of many of Lennie Small's pets whilst in his care of similar injuries, and leads on an incident between him and Mrs Carlson's husband, it appears that he is responsible for her death. What then happened is unclear. Small is thought to have fled the scene, during which the body of Mrs Carlson was discovered by George Milton and fellow worker 'Candy'. George is then thought to have met with Lennie and shot him dead with a revolver. His motives are as yet unclear. Speculations from the ranch suggest that Mr Curley Carlson set off in search of Lennie and that if he had found him before George, Lennie would have been more brutally killed, whilst there is no doubt that if found guilty, he would have been hanged for his crimes. It is unlikely that Milton will be prosecuted and detectives' investigations are likely to continue.

James Hardy (14)
Torquay Boys' Grammar School, Torquay

A Day In The Life Of Lenny
(Inspired by 'Of Mice and Men' by John Steinbeck)

Well, well, I wake up before George so I can pet my pup without him knowing cos George says I shouldn't take 'im outta the pen. Den George says I have to have some water for the workin'. Me an' George den goes and works for da fifty bucks dat we gets an' I buck the barley. I like ta buck barley cos George says I'm good at it. It can get hot so I drink the water an' it cold me dow'.

Afta da workin' George plays on da cards an' I go an' see da pups, they so ... so soft you could pet 'em all day. Den George sometime' normally tells 'bout the place we gonna get, it's gonna be real good an' George says I get ta tend da rabbits, but if I does a bad thin' den I don't get ta tend rabbits so I gonna be good cos I wanna tend da rabbits.

I don't really like the dinner so I pet da pups some more and den George says dat if I don't eat no food, den, den I could die. I don't want dat, cos den I don't get ta tend da rabbits. The sleeping ain't too good cos I think dat da bunks aren't too comfortable. I like ta dream 'bout ma pup and I pet 'im all day long. Dat's really all ma day is on da ranch. I jus' wake up each day an' do it all over again.

Jono Beardsmore (14)
Torquay Boys' Grammar School, Torquay

Of Mice And Men
(Inspired by 'Of Mice and Men' by John Steinbeck)

Last night was hell. Got back from town about four and had a couple of hours sleep. That awful dog stench still hangin' around the bunk house woke me up.

Asked if Lennie was up, he said nofin' but I knew he was awake 'cause I saw him walkin' back from the pup pen couple of minutes ago. All us men in the bunk made it hot an' stuffy an' hard to breathe. Thank God Candy burst through the door.

He shouted us to get up for breakfast, the half who heard was too tired and the ones still asleep weren't movin' either. He grabbed my sheet an' threw it on the floor along with everyone else. All o' us moaned an' groaned 'cause we didn't want t' get up.

Lennie shoved his head in his goddamn bowl, I told him he looked like an animal and he stopped. Everyone was speakin' about the brothel las' night. It was pretty damn expensive, but boy was it good.

We got in teams for horseshoe an' I chucked first, jus' missin' the post. Lennie was out strokin' the pups, probably killin' 'em. Curley was watchin' the match, sittin' down in his goddamn chair with his arm in a sling. The teams were pretty equal goin' into the last game.

Suddenly, Candy came runnin', shoutin' that somethin' was wrong with Curley's wife. We all ran in the barn an' found her dead on the hay. By her side was Lennie's hat, the goddamn fool had killed her!

Joseph Brook (14)
Torquay Boys' Grammar School, Torquay

George ...
(Inspired by 'Of Mice and Men' by John Steinbeck)

It's been two days now ... I jus' keep thinkin' about, well, what I did t' him. I jus' can't get it outta ma' head. I jus' see that big dumb b******'s face every time I close ma eyes ...

I woke that day, ma feet were killin' me. Jus' the other day I had been bucking barley an' swampin' wit' Lennie. I could hear the other guys outside playin' ... oh damn ... what were it called? Horseshoes or summat like that, I never heard or played it before. I thought to maself, *where the hell is Lennie? He better not be with those damn pups or I'll wring his neck t'high hell.*

I went out into the yard an' suddenly Candy comes runnin' out shoutin' at the top o' his voice. I knew Lennie had summat t' do with this, he ain't never not with me. Candy was yellin' for us to run into the barn, we all followed him to where a small, lifeless, limp body lay. I knew at once it were Curley's wife. An' I knew that it were Lennie who killed her, her neck had big red marks around it. I kept tellin' maself that it were gonna be all right, but deep down I knew it weren't ...

Rhys Lewis (14)
Torquay Boys' Grammar School, Torquay

A Day In The Life Of Satan

The brimstone smelled particularly fiery today in Hell. Satan got out of bed and felt cold floor on his feet. He yawned and sparks crackled out of his mouth. He walked out of his bedroom as he put on his red dressing gown. He sniffed the air. 'Ah I love the smell of brimstone in the morning,' sighed Satan happily. 'Better get to work!'

He got dressed in his most menacing cloak. He looked in the mirror and began to shine his horns. He looked at his gleaming horns, 'Perfect,' he said to himself.

He picked up his whip, tucked it into his belt, grabbed his trident and skipped out of the house. The screams of pain hit Satan with incredible force. 'I love my job,' he cried, with an evil grin on his face.

One of his demonic minions ran up to him. 'Sir, Sir, today you will be treating Mr Tarin Reeves,' it said enthusiastically, handing Satan Tarin's Life Folder.

'Thank you my minion,' replied Satan.

'He's in chamber 666,' said the minion, leading Satan to the chamber.

Satan followed, reading the life folder. 'Hmmmm ... his sin was gluttony,' he read aloud.

'He liked his chocolate, Sir!'

'How should I ironically punish him?' pondered Satan.

'You could feed him all the chocolate in the world,' suggested the minion.

'Nah, too over used,' he replied.

'Sorry benevolent master.'

'That's okay, hey I've just had an idea,' cried Satan, 'y'know that pudding Death by Chocolate?'

'That *is* a good idea Sir!'

They reached the chamber, Satan walked in.

'Hello Mr Reeves, d'you like chocolate?'

Jack Staples (13)
Torquay Boys' Grammar School, Torquay

A Day In The Life Of The Grim Reaper

A huge fireball leapt into the air and collided with another which shed a beam of bright light over the clammy, stone-built resting chamber in Hell. This beam woke the Grim Reaper. He picked up his black cloak which totally covered anything below. An unbearable sound erupted from the far side of the room. The Grim Reaper was sharpening his scythe. A silence fell across the chamber as the Grim Reaper raised his hood and placed it on his aged, immortal skull. He picked up the sharpened, wooden scythe and ran his finger bone across the metal blade. A mouth appeared on his skull and it bore an evil grin. A piece of parchment appeared in the Reaper's one free hand and he left the resting chamber. His expression disappeared.

He made his way into the human world, unnoticed. He had three victims in the city of Mosdon, victims of a road accident. He arrived, unnoticed. He took their lives, as if they were toys he could play with. He left, unnoticed. Sixteen more souls waiting to be reaped were resting in Torham General Hospital. The Grim Reaper arrived unnoticed. He knew the man on the second bed. He had visited him six months ago. He had been saved.

The Reaper had a lucky escape. Two thousand victims later and he had cleaned up his city.

He arrived at the Underworld, placed down his scythe, took off his cloak and went to lead his normal life, in a normal world.

Alex Hambis (13)
Torquay Boys' Grammar School, Torquay

Untitled

The boy glanced behind his shoulder, beating the leafless branches out of his way as he fled through the forest. He had been running for an hour now, but he couldn't stop - he knew that if he did they would catch him. He had cuts all over his face, but he couldn't feel a thing, all he could feel was an overwhelming fear of what he had seen.

Finally his body couldn't cope anymore and he collapsed to the floor. He lay there for a while recapping what he'd seen. He knew he couldn't go back, not after all that had happened, he would have to stay in the woods - alone - for eternity.

He had been in the woods for six days now and had just completed his tree house where he would sleep at night. He built it near a river, the water wasn't clean but it would have to do. In the day it was warm, but the trees gave him shade. But at night it was freezing, he would often cover himself in ferns to keep himself warm. He tried to catch fish but soon realised that it wasn't worth the effort. So he lived off berries and mushrooms, he had always liked watching nature programmes on TV.

He heard a gunshot ... then everything went dark ...

Sam Burnham (12)
Torquay Boys' Grammar School, Torquay

A Day In The Life Of An Elf

Elves stay in constant hiding from humans. They live inside trees and bushes, and are five inches tall.

This elf, whose name is Elron, woke up at 4 o'clock on a sunny morning. He clambered up to the top of the tree he lives in and there he found a beehive and took a piece of honeycomb. He clambered back down the tree and crept across the garden that he lived in, to a particularly large bush. Inside this bush was a small, hollowed-out area, in which was a collection of dragonflies.

This was the elves' (or Mirquai as they call themselves) stable tree and all of their dragonflies were kept there. This type of elf travelled on specially bred, trained dragonflies. Elron mounted his emerald-green dragonfly and sped from the bush.

To any watching humans there was just a flash of green as they flew high above houses, heading for the woods nearby. Elron tied up the dragonfly to a small tree near the centre of the woods and headed for a group of enormous oak trees. Elron's job was construction and deep in the forest an elf city was being built. Already there were walkways between the trees and tiny houses were being constructed. Elron took hold of a tamed woodpecker and got to work ...

Tom Colley (12)
Torquay Boys' Grammar School, Torquay

A Day In The Life Of A Football

I'm sitting here now, in the damp, dark shed. I haven't been out in a long, long time. The only sound is the wind outside, and the soft, faint sound of snow hitting the ground. I used to be loved. Back when the sun shone down on me. It was the kind of life fit for a God.

Every morning I would get woken up by my master. He would love me, hug me, but that was the only goodness in it. The next thing I knew, I was hitting the hard ground. I was being kicked around. Sometimes it was just the master, throwing me back and forth against the hard, solid brick wall. It was terrible. But most of the time it was worse than terrible. His so-called 'friends' would torture me until I was sore.

Even if it rained, they would indirectly torture me. They would run for shelter inside their cosy, warm, dry homes. However, I was thrown into a muddy puddle to slowly rot in my state of chill.

It was shocking. It truly was the worst life to live. Not fit for a god, nor a king. My life was not even fit for a very low form of toilet cleaner.

Anyway, there is nothing I can do. I'm lost at the back of the shed. I no longer have a friend in the world. I'm just a lost ball in a world with no love. If only I had just deflated a long, long time ago. There would have been no suffering, no pain in my life.

Joe Vincent (13)
Torquay Boys' Grammar School, Torquay

Hold The Front Page

A meteor of an apocalyptic scale has collided with the Earth, three miles south-west of Land's End in Cornwall. This has triggered a tsunami, hundreds of storeys high. The entire UK and Ireland have been washed away. Severe damage in several countries in Europe along with the entire north-west of Europe under water. Millions are dead, injured or homeless. 'Atlantis', as it is now being called by the press, is calling for aid for those still injured or homeless in the most terrible tragedy in the history of humanity. Across the Atlantic in the Americas, a full scale evacuation is taking place. The main cities in Central and Eastern America have been predicted to be destroyed. As the tsunami hits the Americas and Caribbean, it will pass over Central America and lose momentum where the tsunami will end. America and Europe are asking for aid from some of the poorest countries in the world. By the latest figures, 140 million people have been killed in Europe, 300 million injured or becoming homeless, many people are asking the question, 'Could more have been done to stop this atrocity from happening?' Which the world's governments are answering with a stiff upper lip.

News just coming in as we went to press is that a full-scale alien invasion has been spotted in the atmosphere firing huge laser beams at major cities around the Earth.

Is this the end of the planet as we know it? Only time will tell.

Alex Finn (13)
Torquay Boys' Grammar School, Torquay

A Day In The Life Of A Seagull

This morning I woke up with a splitting headache from when I was hit by a dustbin lid when I was discovered raiding the fish and chip shop bins the day before.

I found myself shut in that same bin, but I couldn't remember how I'd got there. I struggled and rammed and flapped in the bin, but the lid had been welded to the top of the bin and I couldn't get out.

I struggled and flapped some more, without success, so I gave up and started doing what seagulls do best, eating everything in the area. There were plenty of mouldy fish bones and mashed up chips in the bottom of the bin, among tin openers, bent plastic forks and paper drinks cups, mmmm ... mouldy fish bones.

Once I had eaten everything in the bin, I set out pecking at the side of the bin, for it seemed the best thing to do at the time and besides, I might have been able to peck a hole in the bin and escape. As it happened, the bin I was shut in was old and rusty and after about ten minutes of frantic pecking the bin fell apart and I was able to get out.

As soon as I was free I flew back to my nest on the roof of a nearby house, only to find that it had been occupied by another seagull in my absence. I tried to drive him off, but he was bigger and stronger than me and he sent me packing.

I now live in a bush in someone's back garden, not a very good place if you ask me, especially as it is nowhere near the fish and chip shop.

Michael Wilby (12)
Torquay Boys' Grammar School, Torquay

High Security

Jenkins sat at his desk reading the daily reports as usual. Everything seemed to be as it should, everything was fine. As Jenkins made to grab a bottle of whiskey from his secret drawer, Natalie's voice filled the room. 'Sir, it's broken loose!'

'Seal off Room 326,' he barked down the microphone. 'Send the eighth platoon downstairs to guard the door. Send second squadron up to me.'

Jenkins pulled out his bottle of whiskey, it was going to be a long night.

Robert Jenkins had undergone every security drill, but nothing could have prepared him for the real thing. The door slid open, there, silhouetted in the hallway, stood second squadron.

'Sir, are you all right?' asked their leader, who then tossed him a pistol. 'You know how to use one of those things?'

'Just because I'm a scientist, doesn't make me a coward,' replied Jenkins.

'Sir, it's broken through, eighth platoon are down. It's making its way upstairs,' said Natalie.

'How long before it reaches us?' asked Jenkins.

'About ...'

The sound stopped abruptly and the lights went out. Everyone was silent. With the power down, Natalie, the computer artificial intelligence, was unable to use the laboratory's defences. They were on their own. In the silence the heavy footsteps of the thing could be easily heard. It was at the door. Everyone checked their weapons and aimed. The door slid open and they all fired.

Luke Jeffery (13)
Torquay Boys' Grammar School, Torquay

A Day In The Life Of A Coke Can

I was being born. My liquid aluminium form flowed through many pipes and eventually splurted out into the cool factory air and down into my cast. I was moving along a conveyor belt humming a tune to myself when I was rudely interrupted and thrown into a cold room with lots of other aluminium casts. It was all dark. Under the dull throbbing of the cooling fridge I found myself lulled into a deep sleep.

I awoke to find my body had become solid and that I was again rolling along another conveyor belt. The belt stopped and I peered up at the tin tube in front of my face. Without warning it shot out thousands of tiny screaming paint particles so I closed my eyes and rolled over. When I next braved to open my eyes, my body had been spoiled with the Coca-Cola logo. I was all red and had writing all over my back. I bounced around, trying to escape this most torturous way of branding, but something picked me up and filled me with my archenemy, Coke.

I had already been a Coke can before and was well aware of the horrors Coke could cause you. It made your lid itch and your body rot. Overall, you didn't want to be a Coke can, but something more subtle, perhaps a still water can or lemonade, that was often fun.

Harrhy James (13)
Torquay Boys' Grammar School, Torquay

The Story Of Bigfoot

The story of Bigfoot has baffled scientists and people for many years. How can a seemingly ape-like figure roam around on its own in the vast forests of Canada and North America? If the legend is to be proven real then we need pictures, eye witness accounts and maybe we will even need to capture Bigfoot.

Until now scientists have thought that it will be impossible to ever catch Bigfoot in the giant forests. What if Bigfoot is just a man in a suit? According to people that have really seen the legend (or so they say), Bigfoot stands around 11 feet tall and weighs somewhere in the region of 350 pounds. They're all wrong, Bigfoot is no way near that big (although he is quite lanky).

To me Bigfoot comes in the form of Nick Avery, a classmate who acts like Bigfoot and is very dopey. He wanders around like an unevolved caveman, whose only task on this Earth is to look ridiculous. Everywhere he goes people laugh at him but he doesn't care. He's so stupid, he doesn't realise that people are laughing at him, not with him.

So all the people who have dedicated their life to searching the wilds of America and Canada are wasting their time. Bigfoot lives right in the community with people and he doesn't do them any harm (usually).

I will put Bigfoot up for sale at a private auction and prices will start at around £200,000 on the road. Please note that Bigfoot can't really be trusted as a household pet because he isn't very good with children and he has a bad temper.

Henry Irvine (13)
Torquay Boys' Grammar School, Torquay

A Day In The Life Of A Tennis Ball

Whizz ... smack! I was pelted among a large herd of air molecules. They didn't like being hit, so they tried to push me in another direction, but without success. I zoomed past my fellow mates, who were also being punished harshly, by mean-looking giants with four long lumps and a big lump on top. I just missed a lime-coloured stranger - why couldn't everyone be yellow? - Who crashed into a huge metal thing with lots of squares which one of them he stuck into and couldn't get out. As I continued my descent, I was whacked by a huge monster that had lots of square teeth lined up in rows in a massive oval-shaped mouth and a lump sticking out of its head - which might have actually been its head.

I flinched as a huge shock wave vibrated my round body. As it died away, I was once again hurtled through my molecular enemies - the air atoms. But this time I was sent up almost vertically, speeding up as I went along - but what was this? I gradually started to slow down. Ever so suddenly, I stopped. Halted in air. Atoms whacking me in the face - beating me up. I was going back down, to Hell, to doom - where once again, I would be hit, smacked, bullied ... and killed.

Arun Allen (12)
Torquay Boys' Grammar School, Torquay

A Day In The Life Of Michael Vaughan

I woke up early, ready to go for what might be the biggest game I have every played in my entire cricketing career: England vs Australia in the Final Test match to decide who will win The Ashes. The Ashes is the biggest cricketing challenge an England representative will ever face. For years on end Australia have always won the tournament ... the last time England won, was nearly 20 years ago.

The first few weeks have been thrilling; Australia comprehensively won the first two test matches against us before we bounced back with vengeance to win by an innings and 12 runs at Edgbaston. Then we scraped home by 2 wickets at Trent Bridge and now it all comes down to the final game at Lords: the home of cricket.

I was changed and ready to go for 8, I felt wide awake after my poached eggs and toast and drove to Lords for 8.45. I did all of my pre-match rituals nice and early before going to check out the wicket. I desperately needed some runs under my belt; my previous scores in the series had been, 10, 6, 23, 1, 0, 13. I couldn't ask for a better day to score runs: blazing sunshine, blue sky, no wind ... perfect!

I walked out to toss with Aussie skipper Ricky Ponting amid cheers and whistles by the England Barmy Army. *The toss will be crucial,* I thought as I tossed the coin. Ponting called tails, it was heads. First blood to us as I informed him we would stick the pads on, I felt like opening, maybe it would put my run of bad scores to an end.

The tension was building, it had been building for the last two hours. Finally the umpires gave us the nod and me and Andrew Strauss walked out to bat. My stomach had turned upside down as I walked out, but as I approached the crease I strangely seemed calm. Who knows what would happen next? As the fastest bowler in the world, Brett Lee, ran in to bowl the first ball to me, I had the hopes of England on my shoulders ...

Matt Thompson (13)
Torquay Boys' Grammar School, Torquay

12-Year-Old Protests Atop Wind Singer
(Inspired by 'The Wind Singer' by William Nicholson)

Kestrel Hath of Orange District, the day before yesterday, on top of the Wind Singer protested against everything this city knows and stands for.

After having her rating lowered in school, she proceeded at break to the Wind Singer, where she shouted anti-social comments, including her denial of the existence of the Emperor!

Many hours later, after much coaxing from librarian father Hanno, she climbed down and went home.

Neighbour of the Hath family, Mrs M Blesh talked to us about it: 'Well, it's just disgraceful, I mean the things she said, some of them were just terrible. Saying we don't have an Emperor'. At this point the interview concluded, as the shocked Mrs Blesh, mother of two, broke down in tears.

We were denied an interview with Chief Examiner, Maslo Inch, but from a statement made by Government spokesman, Alvadat Misc, we understand that sometime during yesterday's meeting between Maslo Inch and Kestrel and Hanno Hath, Kestrel escaped.

Her mother, Ira, descendent of the great prophetess, Ira Manth, told officials that she had absolutely no idea where her daughter could be.

For the next 12 days, Government trackers will search the entire city for her. After this period, she will be presumed missing and if not found within 6 months after this, will be officially declared dead.

William Saunders (12)
Torquay Boys' Grammar School, Torquay

The Hath Family Shame Orange!

(Inspired by 'The Wind Singer' by William Nicholson)

Yesterday in Orange District an atrocity occurred, Hanno Hath and his family were demoted to Grey District, all thanks to their eldest daughter Kestrel and her disgraceful acts around the Wind Singer. Hanno Hath is being sent off to a special learning centre where he can learn to do better in the high examination. It's a wonder they ever got as far as Orange. Many families turned up yesterday when Ira Hath, her son Bowman and her youngest daughter Pinpin packed in preparation to leave their house in Orange.

Many thought that the family would only be demoted the one colour, but no, they go all the way to Grey! The new family to move in is the Davil family, who we all hope will have many more friends than the Hath family and someday be moved to Maroon.

As people turned up, waiting for the Haths to move out Bowman, Ira's son, shouted out, 'Run Kestrel, run'. This caused everyone to turn around and stare at the figure who could only be Kestrel Hath.

All at once the guards charge after her, but one guard, as he later recalls, heard baby Pinpin shout, 'Kestrel', and then he saw Bowman and Kestrel run out of the house down a back alley. The guard chased after them but Kestrel and Bowman were hiding somewhere.

Meanwhile back at the Hath's old house 'Kestrel' had been caught but was uncovered only to find a grinning Mumpo underneath! How had she changed places? Where was she? Now the more important question is where is she now?

This report was compiled by the director of the Weekly Exam, James Sutherland.

James Sutherland (12)
Torquay Boys' Grammar School, Torquay

Crazy Kestrel And Boy Bowman Go Missing!

(Inspired by 'The Wind Singer' by William Nicholson)

On Sunday 18th March 2594, two family members left home. Their mother quotes, 'They have gone for a reason, but I can't explain why'.

The whole village isn't mournful, but very pleased. They said that the children caused too much trouble. A man said, 'Kestrel fled because moving from Orange to Grey District was a bit too hard'.

Mr Policeman from the police department declared, 'An impostor caught all of our attention, but I really saw Kestrel running in the opposite direction'. This may mean that there is a *third member!* Maybe there are more than three!

The old children complained, 'We tried to stop them, we promise. But they didn't want to come with us. About a day later we saw them in the desert, then we surrounded them, but they are so lucky, a big tall thing came by and took them away'.

This amazing news means that they are alive, but heading up to the 'Crack in the Land'. How long will the twins and the impostor survive? To find out, read next week's headliner!

Jonathan Munro (12)
Torquay Boys' Grammar School, Torquay

Disgrace To The Hath Family

(Inspired by 'The Wind Singer' by William Nicholson)

Yesterday morning the high examination took place. The Hath family took 2-year-old Pinpin to her examination. The Hath family were embarrassed as they had failed the examination yet again!

This is what Mr Hath had to say, 'We are really ashamed not to be promoted. We have not been promoted in years. I am worried that if we do not get promoted soon we will end up being demoted'.

Pinpin, 2, did not have a clue what was going on. In the examination she could not count, did not talk and she was not clean.

Kestrel, 14, did not want to go and Bowman, also 14, was sad and felt sorry for Pinpin. All of the family hoped and prayed that Pinpin might finally get them promoted.

The Blesh family got promoted. This is what Mr Blesh had to say about Hanno Hath: 'Hanno really needs to sort out his family. If he does not, they will end up being demoted'.

David Burke (11)
Torquay Boys' Grammar School, Torquay

She's Got Nerves
(Inspired by 'The Wind Singer' by William Nicholson)

Young hooligan, Kestrel Hath, went missing three days ago following a terrible offence she committed the Thursday before. Along with Kestrel, twin brother Bowman and Classmate Mumpo went missing the same day. The twins' parents yesterday issued a speech on national TV.

Ira Hath said, 'If anyone knows where our daughter and son are, contact the police immediately, I'm begging you'.

The father of the twins, Hanno, then added without hesitation, 'Darlings, we're not angry with you. Please come home'.

As Mumpo does not have any parents, no speech was made for him.

Kestrel Hath, on Thursday, committed the crime of all crimes: she made a show of Aramanth, the Emperor and the rating system.

Using words that couldn't possibly be mentioned, for all our sakes, she said that Aramanth was stupid, the Emperor doesn't exist and the rating system doesn't work. She managed to say all of this on the top of a high building in front of many people, including young children.

One policeman said, 'Due to the size of Aramanth, it's impossible to have a guess where they are'.

The police don't believe that the terrible trio could have left Aramanth. The Hath family had been relegated from the Orange District on the day that Kestrel, Bowman and Mumpo went missing. Ira, Hanno and toddler, Pinpin, are now settling in at the Grey District.

'People are always making comments, or giving us nasty looks', says Ira Hath. 'It's just not fair', Ira quickly added.

Jordan Bright (12)
Torquay Boys' Grammar School, Torquay

Kestrel Kills The Old Queen
(Inspired by 'The Wind Singer by William Nicholson)

Kestrel Hath visited the old queen with her brother and disgusting friend called Mumpo, and scared the life out of the fragile, wrinkly, dying, tired queen. Her brother, Bowman, messed with her feelings, using black magic.

The three witches will hurt old people, mud people and all types of living creatures on their quest to find the Wind Singer. They will have to go through all sorts of other terrains and fight creatures, riding anything they can to get to their destination and do their evil deeds.

They caused havoc in their town by escaping in a chase and causing trouble at school. They were moved down to the Grey District, and Hanno Hath was put in a training school to learn to honour his family better. Kestrel ran out of school and climbed the Wind Singer and shouted, 'Sagahog badoodle'.

The band of kids went through all sorts of places before running in on the Queen's day-care centre and watching the children planning how they would cook them. The 'kids' then burst in on the oldest person and startled her.

Gordon Watton (12)
Torquay Boys' Grammar School, Torquay

Disgraceful Girl Clambers To The Wind Singer
(Inspired by 'The Wind Singer' by William Nicholson)

Yesterday, Aramanth was disgraced at the sight of a young girl climbing up the tower which holds the Wind Singer. At the top, the girl shouted, 'Pongo to exams'.

Kestrel, a young girl who lives in Orange District, started the day with her baby sister doing her first ever exam. She failed miserably.

Later, Kestrel had an argument with her teacher and sat at the back of the class when she was told not to. This was not a good start to the day.

Many people think this was disgraceful behaviour and no one should ever do this again. Maslo Inch explained to The Moon, 'I am truly disgraced by the behaviour of this mad girl. I went to school with her father and I never guessed that he would have such a badly-behaved child. They will definitely move down to Grey District if this behaviour is repeated, and might well be moving down to Maroon now. I will be having strong words and plead with her to stop behaving like this'.

Meanwhile, a fellow neighbour of the Hath family told us, 'I totally agree that the way Aramanth is run is disgraceful. The exams, rankings and rules are totally stupid, but I still do not think the way the girl acted was acceptable'.

Here at the centre of Aramanth, everyone is talking about the actions of one small girl who lives in Orange District. The Hath family are all very embarrassed.

Luke Hayward (12)
Torquay Boys' Grammar School, Torquay

The Mudnut Harvest

(Inspired by 'The Wind Singer' by William Nicholson)

The mudnut harvest took place in the Underlake at dawn, yesterday. The gorgeous mudnut, was harvested all morning by the Mud People.

Mudnuts are buried under the rind in the salt caves. The Mud People take them out at an astonishing 5 mudnuts per second! Children then take them to be roasted.

Miss Bundlebluff quoted, 'A roasted mudnut has a lovely flavour, creamy and roasted'.

Three Skinnies left the salt cave yesterday to get the Wind Singer's voice. I hope they don't mind the strange old children.

A diving sport also took place on that special day. The sport consists of a high pole, watery mud and, of course, a loud audience! Mud People jump off the pole into the mud. The winner is the person who stays under the longest. Mumpo was the winner yesterday!

Anthony Savage (12)
Torquay Boys' Grammar School, Torquay

Bowman, Kestrel And Mumpo Escape Aramanth

(Inspired by 'The Wind Singer' by William Nicholson)

In an amazing act of shame and stupidity, Bowman and Kestrel Hath and Mumpo have fled from Aramanth, escaping into the Underlake.

The Hath family: mum, Ira; dad, Hanno and children Bowman, Kestrel and Pinpin, had been demoted from Orange District to Maroon because Kestrel Hath had climbed to the top of the Wind Singer and shouted down one of the leather horns. It took the marshals five hours to get her down. The chief examiner took her and Hanno to talk to them and to show them the Underlake, the ultimate punishment, but Kestrel fell into the muddy sewage. She managed to climb out and jump onto the examiner's shoulders and started to throttle him.

Later, Kestrel and Bowman ran away into the Underlake, where the Mud People have allegedly attacked them. Minutes later, Mumpo ran in, thinking he could save them. They have never come out. This, we think, is reason to believe that they have been killed or eaten.

We spoke to Ira Hath and she bravely said, 'I am very worried about them, but I am sure I will see them again soon'.

The Hath family have been demoted to the Grey District as a result of their children running away.

Peter Dawkins (11)
Torquay Boys' Grammar School, Torquay

Crazy Girl Climbs The Wind Singer
(Inspired by 'The Wind Singer' by William Nicholson)

News just in: a small girl that belongs to the Hath family, apparently called Kestrel, has decided to rebel against Aramanth and has climbed to the top of the Wind Singer. The army, SWAT team and the police are trying to persuade Kestrel to come down from the top of the Wind Singer. Not only that, but paramedics are on standby, just in case something develops.

John Richards (12)
Torquay Boys' Grammar School, Torquay

A Day In The Life Of A Millipede

I was walking along the street when a UFO came and beamed me up. In a flash of light, I was in a giant world. Every tree was the size of three of Earth's tallest skyscrapers.

When I moved, it struck me what I was. I was a millipede. I practised walking and it was horribly hard. When I was walking along, the ground swallowed me up! I was with thousands of ants.

I walked for miles along tunnels, then the ground caved in again and I was in a cave with a pillar in it. Then the pillar snapped and the ceiling caved in. I ran for miles along an exit tunnel to the surface.

Then I climbed to the very top of a tree. It was so tiring, climbing a vertical angle for miles, with thousands of legs. When I got to the top, I lay there, then a hawk came along, which was the size of a jumbo jet. It snatched me in its beak and took me away. It was a weird feeling, being hundreds of miles up. I managed to wriggle out of its beak. Suddenly, I was falling for miles.

In an instant, the UFO came, beamed me up and beamed me down as a human, with my memory of it erased.

John Ware (11)
Torquay Boys' Grammar School, Torquay

Rockwell Farm

The spaceship landed, Cypto jumped out summarising his environment. Posc, his alien leader, spoke from the mothership.

'Cypto, your mission is to destroy all humans.'

Cypto had landed on a farm. He wandered over to the cows, thinking these were the dominant life form on Earth. 'Hello, Earthling, your planet has been invaded,' said Cypto.

The cow stared back at him, confused, then turned round with her rear end in Cytpo's face, and let one rip.

'I don't care how many stomachs you have!' shouted Cypto angrily. Then he drew out his ray gun and vaporised the cow.

Cypto wandered up to a house. Out came Farmer Rockwell.

'I didn't know we were having steak for dinner,' the farmer said, confused. 'That's not a steak, it's a green monkey. Martha, get me the shotgun.'

'I am not green,' replied Cypto. Then, using his brain probe, Cypto extracted Farmer Rockwell's brain.

'Cypto, get to your ship and destroy them,' said Posc.

Cypto ran back to his ship, beamed himself into it and took off. He hovered over to the nearest barn and using his destructo ray, melted it to pieces.

Suddenly, a large bullet pierced the saucer and sent it crashing down. The saucer plunged down and plunged to the ground. When Cypto emerged, he was surrounded by the army.

'Surrender, you green ... thing,' said the general, unsure of what to say.

'I am not green,' replied Cypto angrily. Then he exploded, and only green goo remained.

Luke Lake (12)
Torquay Boys' Grammar School, Torquay

Tom Bond

Tom ducked behind the wall as the missile flew overhead. He was only 15, but had seen more than many adults would in a lifetime. Knives in heads, bullet wounds punching through a body; a grim life, but he had to do it. His parents had died in a boat crash; it was not by coincidence. A highly paid assassin had rigged a bomb to go off at 7.50. At 7.50, they were halfway up the gangplank and were blasted to atoms. Now he was on the run from the Mafia. He had stopped them twice now, they couldn't tolerate this, and from a child? Definitely not.

Bullets smashed into the top of the wall; he crouched lower. The gunfire ceased. He looked up and they had gone, or so he thought. Two jeeps raced through the school gates, men with AKs pounding round after round at him. He still held the card that he had found on one of the men. It resembled a key card, but in fact was the key to 200 nuclear bombs just waiting to go off. He screamed as a round caught his arm. Blood spurted out and his white shirt was stained red. The jeeps had raced past and were coming in for the kill. Tom couldn't take any more. He picked up a pole lying broken next to him and lunged at the nearest driver, breaking his nose. The man shot and caught him in the chest. He flew backwards, unconscious.

Michael Barrington (12)
Torquay Boys' Grammar School, Torquay

The Bogie Man Vs Mr Grim!

'Get over here, or I'll shoot you with my bogializer!' said the Bogie Man.

'Never!' bellowed Mr Grim as he lay on the floor with a bogie stuck to each side of his face.

Crack, smash, boom.

'Let's get out of here,' said the Bogie Man as the middle part of the roof fell down.

'Argh! My back!' screamed Mr Grim.

Then there was a flash of light and both Mr Grim and the Bogie Man covered their eyes. Then, when the brightness had gone, they pulled their hands away from their faces to discover a great, gold hole hovering in front of them. Suddenly, they both looked at each other and charged towards the opening. They stopped for a second and then dived in. It was like a slide going on and on, and then it vanished and they both fell to the ground.

Where are we?' squeaked Mr Grim.

'I dunno, but I still wanna kill you!' bellowed the Bogie Man in an outraged voice.

Peow, peow. 'Got ya!'

Bang, bang.

'No, no the mirror, don't reflect it!' said the trembling Bogie Man.

'Argh, you stupid ball of snot!' yelled Mr Grim.

'I'm getting out of here and I'm not taking you with me,' said the Bogie Man as he rode off into the distance.

Nick Aitchison (12)
Torquay Boys' Grammar School, Torquay

Rocky Goes To France

Rocky was to board the ferry at Plymouth and had just handed in his passport. He then waddled out and gazed up at the magnificent ferry. When he got on board, he sprinted to the cinema and went to watch a film.

Hours later, he came out and went for something to eat, but on his way, he saw three men trying to hijack the ship. At that exact moment, Rocky brought out his cape and used his powers. *Rocky Bottom!* After getting them, he kicked them overboard and ran to the captain's quarters. When he got there, he found the captain tied up and not breathing. Rocky knew what he had to do. It was his responsibility to sail to France.

When Rocky arrived in France, he got a funny little French hat and some cheese. He sat there all night, eating cheese and fighting crime.

Adam Robinson (12)
Torquay Boys' Grammar School, Torquay

A Day In The Life Of George Milton
(Inspired by 'Of Mice and Men' by John Steinbeck)

He didn't mean to do it. Did he? Well, it's his fault if we are stuck in this ditch. Hell, I am too scared to move a muscle as I hear the pounding hooves of horses an' the piercing growls of dogs. There are two thoughts going through my mind: *I'm cold,* an', *why the hell am I staying with this large fellow with no mind of his own?*

Now's our chance and we run. We run until our legs can carry us no more.

'George, where are we goin'?' Lennie whispers.

'Far away,' I reply.

Lennie quickly takes a small, soft object from his pocket.

'Lennie, what's tha ...' I shout.

'Er, nothing,' Lennie replies.

'For God's sake, drop that dead mouse.'

Lennie, why the hell do I stay with you?

'Jesus Christ, you're a crazy b******d. If I was alone, I could live so easy. I could go and get a job an' jus' grab my money at the end of the month. But what I got? I got you! You can't get no job an' you lose me ever' job I get.' The fury from my face drops as I see Lennie. He can't help himself.

Lennie shyly stutters, 'I, I'll go live in a cave, George, an', an' live off berries an' stuff.'

Suddenly I feel sorry for him. He looks like a little scared kid an' I think, *what the hell, someone has to look after this dumb guy, haven't they?* Well it looks like Lennie and I will always be stuck together. Jus' me an' 'im.

Chris Gossage (14)
Torquay Boys' Grammar School, Torquay

A Day In The Life Of George

(Inspired by 'Of Mice and Men' by John Steinbeck)

The sun was slowly rising on the horizon, and with it, bringing the great blanket of heat that lay across the fields on which the people on the ranch have to work. Along with the sunrise came light and the awakening of George.

'Another day, another dime,' said George. George gave a huge yawn as he dragged himself out of bed.

'Lennie!' shouted George, intending to wake up the big baby that laid in the bed above him. 'Lennie, wake up, ya big, blubberin' fool!'

Lennie slowly opened his eyes to see where he was and who was shouting. He turned around, got down from his bed and sat on a chair with his head in his hands.

George walked outside and prepared for a day's work. He went to go and wash his face to wake up more, and as he did, he could feel the intense heat rising off the ground.

A few minutes later, Lenny joined him outside and started to have a wash.

'Make sure you drink a lot today, Lennie,' said George.

Lennie replied with a mumble which, only if you listened carefully, came out to be, 'OK George.'

They both then had something to eat and started their day's work. Just as George had suspected, the heat was intense, everybody was so hot. At the end of the day's work, George was describing their cottage and with that ended one of many days they had on the ranch, with many more to come.

Harry Richardson (14)
Torquay Boys' Grammar School, Torquay

Rabid Girl Rampages
(Inspired by 'The Wind Singer' by William Nicholson)

Kestral Hath, 15, of Orange District, has been sought after by the wardens and examiners for two days. On Friday the 16th May, she was spotted by a warden, but the incompetent Pocksriker was too slow and failed to bring her in.

Kestrel is wanted for blasphemy, as she escaped from school on the 12th May and shouted unspeakable utterings through the Wind Singer, which amplified it so the whole city could hear. When she is captured, the Old Manth Herald expects Kestrel will go to Special Teaching, as the chief examiner sees no hope. Here is a direct quote from our interview with Marlo Inch, 'Well, the girl is utterly mad, clearly, and must be put down before people follow her example. If you find Kestrel in your house, approach with extreme caution. To be honest, it is her parents' fault; they see no reason to strive harder'. I think this just about sums up all our news.

Well to summarise, remember to catch her if seen, and not help her! Remember, capture may lead to a reward of points, so get busy.

Matt Scott (12)
Torquay Boys' Grammar School, Torquay

Old People Attack
(Inspired by 'The Wind Singer' by William Nicholson)

At exactly 2.36pm, 24th April 2005, in Aramanth, a terrible thing happened. Three people, named Kestrel Hath, Bowman Hath and Mumpo had a horrific fright.

The three people had just left the salt caves, with some food given by the Mud People to keep them going, and were heading home. All three of them had walked miles and miles, until they saw an object in the distance. As they got to the object, they studied it and found out that it was an abandoned sailing ship. They sheltered behind it for a while, because the wind was blowing at horrific speed.

After resting for a while, Kestrel noticed some figures. As she and the other two watched them coming closer and closer, they knew that they were the old people straight away.

A witness, who at the time of the incident was flying a helicopter said, 'There were so many of these people, in rings of approximately 250, edging in on the innocent people. It was frightening to look at'. This witness was the one who called the Aramanthiana police.

Daniel Garswood (12)
Torquay Boys' Grammar School, Torquay

Death

Death is an odd creature. Basically, a skeleton wearing a long black robe with a hood to cover his shiny, ivory-like skull. He is normally seen by those who are to die. A scythe is his weapon of choice held by his claw-shaped hands. These too are as white as snow. Death is feared by those who know nothing of him, who are too awestruck at his sight, to believe in him. They see his tall, dark, foreboding figure and double-take. They play with their minds, *no, he can't be there; it's just my imagination. If I ignore him he'll go away.*

Another of Death's features is his eyes. Red, pearly lasers staring at the eyes of the beholder. Almost jewel-like, they are the only thing that can be seen under his hood. He is possibly the most feared creature in the upper lands.

Not many people know about Death's transportation. This must be faster than the speed of light for Death to succeed in his work. For this he chooses a creature know to many to be a myth, non-existent. A creature who can fly far distances and have its own defence. A creature known as a dragon. Death's dragon has no particular name but his master refers to it as Ebony. Ebony - king of all skies.

'Faster, Ebony, faster! Show these skies their master,' Death said, with a voice like nails on a blackboard. The dragon dived down into the clouds like a knife through butter, its large, scaly wings testing the limits.

Ebony twirled round gracefully, shooting fire in a jet of light. Death peered down at the mountains of Nirathall and grinned menacingly.

'Down there, Ebony,' he whispered, 'Tralin will be waiting.'

Gareth Jones (13)
Torquay Boys' Grammar School, Torquay

One Thing

Every child does something that they have been firmly told not to do. Often, it is a lot of little things, but sometimes the child only does one. This is when all the disobedience is built up into one thing. That one thing is often something that the child should never do.

The little girl was one of those cases. One thing. She might have gone on to do more than one thing, but she could not. Not after this.

The girl's only rebellion was entering the forest. She thought that nothing could go wrong. If there were animals in the dark forest, then surely she would have heard them. If there were no animals in the forest, then there was nothing that could kill her. However, what the girl did not know was that there were no animals; no squirrels, no birds, no mice. There was only one thing, breathing in the forest.

This thing in the woods did try to avoid having to kill the girl. It gave the whole forest a sweet smell. Not sugar sweet, but sickly sweet. The smell of death. It tried to scare her away. It howled, telling her that she had made a mistake. There was life in the forest. The girl would not listen. She walked straight into the thing's territory, unaware that none had left since the monster had entered. Now that she was in there, she was not afraid. Nothing would make her leave or that was what she thought. The truth was that nothing would let her leave.

Matthew Thornton (13)
Torquay Boys' Grammar School, Torquay

The Sunday Singer
(Inspired by 'The Wind Singer' by William Nicholson)

I've been to the land of the Mud People! Yesterday, after recovering from shock, a young girl whose name has yet to be released, gave the Aramanth police this statement. 'I have been to the land of the Mud People! I have watched them diving into the mud of the Underlake. I have slept in their beds and I have eaten their food, yet I am still alive. These are gentle beings who would risk their own lives to save any one of ours!' She went on describing the Mud People until she finally had to stop, due to her unstable condition.

She has given detailed descriptions of the food, living quarters and the habits of the Mud People, and helped the people of Aramanth to learn that little bit extra about the secret people.

A picture of a Mud Man shows him standing next to the Underlake. As you can see, they wear little clothing and they are covered in hair. They are also said to be around 4ft 2 inches.

Max Leaman (12)
Torquay Boys' Grammar School, Torquay

Blood Has Never Tasted Better!

I felt the dark curtain of the night get drawn over the sky. Brilliant! Time to get up. I'm a vampire, you see, and my day begins now.

I lifted my coffin lid. It opened with a slow crescendoing creak. My mouth was ravenous for blood; human blood.

I slowly crept out of the dark depths of my lair. It's an abandoned, old, middle ages church. Not many people like to wander around churches and graveyards in the middle of the night, so I quickly darted across to the nearest house and my normal source of tasty, thick blood. Mr Raven.

Now getting closer, my mouth was watering. I was getting ever closer by the second. My mouth was howling out of thirst. I stepped up to the door. Ha ... poor old Mr Raven falls for it every time. *Knock! Knock!* From my previous visits, I knew he'd still be up at this time. I heard his smelly bare feet lift up and down as he trudged towards the door.

The handle turned slightly round on the old cottage door, then slightly more. *Click!* He pushed it open. I couldn't wait any longer to plunge my starving fangs into his awaiting neck. I recognised his bewildered face. Finally I could feast.

Being a vampire, you have to make sure you don't take too much blood by getting carried away. Mr Raven's blood was better than ever, it almost tasted of raspberry ripple flavour!

I left him back in his chair, so he would wake up just as normal. Addiction overwhelmed me, so I rushed away for more!

Sam Hurst (12)
Torquay Boys' Grammar School, Torquay

A Day In The Life Of Jim Bob Marley

Beep, beep, beep, beep, beep, beep, goes the alarm. Jim bangs the alarm clock, pulls away the covers and gets out of bed. He pulls on his rough clothes, combs his thick hair and walks to the door, where he takes out his gun and checks for bullets. Jim finally unlocks the front door, walks outside and steps into his mucky Volvo.

Jim Bob Marley is an old-aged farmer who every day gets up at 6am to shoot foxes to keep them off his beloved farm. He lives on his own on Dartmoor in the middle of nowhere.

Jim eventually arrives at the end of the long track from his house. He immediately gets out of his car. Marley hides behind some bushes, after leaving some food by the bins.

Eventually, after seeing no foxes, Bob heads to his Volvo when suddenly, he hears a noise from the bins. 'Gotcha,' he whispers. He turns around with his gun ready to shoot. *Bang, bang,* two shots are fired. But no, it was not Jim who fired the gun, as the fox was not actually a fox. It was a robber! A robber had killed Jim!

The murderer acts quickly. He grabs Jim by the legs and drags him up the rocky path to Jim's house, where he burns him down to ashes.

The robber got away, so the murder was never discovered. Jim had no friends, so no one bothered to check up on him.

Simon White (13)
Torquay Boys' Grammar School, Torquay